CRIMINAL
INVESTIGATIONS

BANK ROBBERY

CRIMINAL INVESTIGATIONS

CRIMINAL INVESTIGATIONS

BANK ROBBERY

$\underline{v} = x \left(G \right) 0$

MICHAEL NEWTON

Consulting Editor: **JOHN L. FRENCH,**

CRIME SCENE SUPERVISOR,
BALTIMORE POLICE CRIME LABORATORY

CHELSEA HOUSE
PUBLISHERS
An imprint of Infobase Publishing

CRIMINAL INVESTIGATIONS: Bank Robbery

Chelsea House
An imprint of Infobase Publishing
132 West 31st Street
New York NY 10001

Library of Congress Cataloging-in-Publication Data
Newton, Michael, 1951-
Bank robbery / Michael Newton ; consulting editor, John L. French.
p. cm. — (Criminal investigations)
Includes bibliographical references and index.
ISBN-13: 978-0-7910-9401-3 (alk. paper)
ISBN-10: 0-7910-9401-4 (alk. paper)
1. Bank robberies—United States. 2. Brigands and robbers—United States. 3. Thieves—United States. I. French, John L. II. Title. III. Series.
HV6658.N44 2008   364.15′520973—dc22
2008010671

Chelsea House books are available at special discounts when purchased in bulk quantities for businesses, associations, institutions, or sales promotions. Please call our Special Sales Department in New York at (212) 967-8800 or (800) 322-8755.

You can find Chelsea House on the World Wide Web at http://www.chelseahouse.com

Text design by Erika K. Arroyo
Cover design by Ben Peterson

Cover: Safe deposit vault in bank.

Printed in the United States of America

Bang EJB 10 9 8 7 6 5 4 3 2 1

This book is printed on acid-free paper.

All links and Web addresses were checked and verified to be correct at the time of publication. Because of the dynamic nature of the Web, some addresses and links may have changed since publication and may no longer be valid.

Contents

Foreword

In 2000 there were 15,000 murders in the United States. During that same year about a half million people were assaulted, 1.1 million cars were stolen, 400,000 robberies took place, and more than 2 million homes and businesses were broken into. All told, in the last year of the twentieth century, there were more than 11 million crimes committed in this country.*

In 2000 the population of the United States was approximately 280 million people. If each of the above crimes happened to a separate person, only 4 percent of the country would have been directly affected. Yet everyone is in some way affected by crime. Taxes pay patrolmen, detectives, and scientists to investigate it, lawyers and judges to prosecute it, and correctional officers to watch over those convicted of committing it. Crimes against businesses cause prices to rise as their owners pass on the cost of theft and security measures installed to prevent future losses. Tourism in cities, and the money it brings in, may rise and fall in part due to stories about crime in their streets. And every time someone is shot, stabbed, beaten, or assaulted, or when someone is jailed for having committed such a crime, not only they suffer but so may their friends, family, and loved ones. Crime affects everyone.

It is the job of the police to investigate crime with the purpose of putting the bad guys in jail and keeping them there, hoping thereby to punish past crimes and discourage new ones. To accomplish this a police officer has to be many things: dedicated, brave, smart, honest, and imaginative. Luck helps, but it's not required. And there's one more virtue that should be associated with law enforcement. A good police officer is patient.

Patience is a virtue in crime fighting because police officers and detectives know something that most criminals don't. It's not a secret, but most lawbreakers don't learn it until it is too late. Criminals who make money robbing people, breaking into houses, or stealing cars; who live by dealing drugs or committing murder; who spend their days on the wrong side of the law, or commit any other crimes, must remember this: a criminal has to get away with every crime he or she commits. However, to get criminals off the street and put them behind bars, the police only have to catch a criminal once.

The methods by which police catch criminals are varied. Some are as old as recorded history and others are so new that they have yet to be tested in court. One of the first stories in the Bible is of murder, when Cain killed his brother Abel (Genesis 4:1–16). With few suspects to consider and an omniscient detective, this was an easy crime to solve. However, much later in that same work, a young man named Daniel steps in when a woman is accused of an immoral act by two elders (Daniel 13:1–63). By using the standard police practice of separating the witnesses before questioning them, he is able to arrive at the truth of the matter.

From the time of the Bible to almost present day, police investigations did not progress much further than questioning witnesses and searching the crime scene for obvious clues as to a criminal's identity. It was not until the late 1800s that science began to be employed. In 1879 the French began to use physical measurements and later photography to identify repeat offenders. In the same year a Scottish missionary in Japan used a handprint found on a wall to exonerate a man accused of theft. In 1892 a bloody fingerprint led Argentine police to charge and convict a mother of killing her children, and by 1905 Scotland Yard had convicted several criminals thanks to this new science.

Progress continued. By the 1920s scientists were using blood analysis to determine if recovered stains were from the victim or suspect, and the new field of firearms examination helped link bullets to the guns that fired them.

Nowadays, things are even harder on criminals, when by leaving behind a speck of blood, dropping a sweat-stained hat, or even taking a sip from a can of soda, they can give the police everything they need to identify and arrest them.

In the first decade of the twenty-first century the main tools used by the police include

- questioning witnesses and suspects
- searching the crime scene for physical evidence
- employing informants and undercover agents
- investigating the whereabouts of previous offenders when a crime they've been known to commit has occurred
- using computer databases to match evidence found on one crime scene to that found on others or to previously arrested suspects
- sharing information with other law enforcement agencies via the Internet
- using modern communications to keep the public informed and enlist their aid in ongoing investigations

But just as they have many different tools with which to solve crime, so too do they have many different kinds of crime and criminals to investigate. There is murder, kidnapping, and bank robbery. There are financial crimes committed by con men who gain their victim's trust or computer experts who hack into computers. There are criminals who have formed themselves into gangs and those who are organized into national syndicates. And there are those who would kill as many people as possible, either for the thrill of taking a human life or in the horribly misguided belief that it will advance their cause.

The Criminal Investigations series looks at all of the above and more. Each book in the series takes one type of crime and gives the reader an overview of the history of the crime, the methods and motives behind it, the people who have committed it, and the means by which these people are caught and punished. In this series celebrity crimes will be discussed and exposed. Mysteries that have yet to be solved will be presented. Readers will discover the truth about murderers, serial killers, and bank robbers whose stories have become myths and legends. These books will explain how criminals can separate a person from his hard-earned cash, how they prey on the weak and helpless, what is being done to stop them, and what one can do to help prevent becoming a victim.

John L. French,
Crime Scene Supervisor,
Baltimore Police Crime Laboratory

* Federal Bureau of Investigation. "Uniform Crime Reports, Crime in the United States 2000." Available online. URL: http://www.fbi.gov/ucr/00cius.htm. Accessed January 11, 2008.

Introduction

Popular legend claims that bandit Willie Sutton (1901–80), when asked to explain why he robbed banks, replied, "That's where the money is." Sutton himself denied making that statement, but it captures the motive for thousands of safecrackers, armed robbers, and hackers who have looted banks throughout America over the past 210 years. During this time, certain bank robbers have emerged as the nation's most colorful outlaws, elevated by the media and Hollywood to a status approaching hero worship.

Early American bank heists, from the first on record (1798) through the Civil War, were executed by burglars who tunneled and blasted their way into vaults when banks were closed. A new breed of bandits, led by the James and Younger brothers, pioneered daylight bank robbery in February 1866. That holdup launched the James-Younger gang on a 10-year crime spree and spawned many imitators.

While scattered holdup gangs remained active over the next four decades—the Newton brothers established a national record for successful bank jobs in the 1920s—it wasn't until the Great Depression (1929–1941) that a new generation of nationally famous outlaws emerged: John Dillinger, "Baby Face" Nelson, "Pretty Boy" Floyd, "Machine Gun" Kelly, and others. Many Americans rejoiced as bandits robbed the banks that had foreclosed on farms and homes, but a backlash from the Kansas City Massacre of 1933 launched a federal war on crime, spearheaded by J. Edgar Hoover's Federal Bureau of Investigation (FBI).

By 1937 the most famous bandits were dead or in prison, but robbery remains a costly problem for American banks. New federal laws and high-profile pursuit of "public enemies" have failed to eliminate bank robbery as a class of major crime in the United States.

In fact, while no bank bandits have received "star" billing from the media since Willie Sutton's arrest in 1952, holdups are more common than ever before. The FBI reported 8,372 bank robberies nationwide in 1997 (with 40 persons killed), declining slightly to 7,546 in 2000, then increasing in the early years of the twenty-first century. Bank robberies in New York City tripled between 2001 and 2003 (with 408 in the latter year), while Los Angeles suffered 537 in 2004.

Bank Robbery tracks the history of American bandits from their early days to the present, with focus on some of the most notorious offenders. This book also surveys methods used by law enforcement to prevent bank holdups or to capture those responsible.

Chapter 1, "Blood and Money," examines America's first—and still most famous—bank-robbing gang, led by brothers Frank and Jesse James after the Civil War.

Chapter 2, "Manhunters," describes efforts to prevent and punish bank robbery on the American frontier through private police agencies.

Chapter 3, "Lawless Years," reviews the outlaw heyday of 1918–1930, and the measures taken by police to combat roving, well-armed gangs.

Chapter 4, "Gangbusters," visits the "open cities" where corrupt police and politicians welcomed bandits and other fugitives during the Great Depression.

Chapter 5, "Public Enemy No. 1," traces the short and violent career of John Dillinger, the only American outlaw whose fame rivals that of Jesse James.

Chapter 6, "Where the Money Is," explores the methods of Willie Sutton, a bank robber whose crimes spanned nearly half a century.

Chapter 7, "Most Wanted," surveys the FBI's Ten Most Wanted list, highlighting some notorious cases and evaluating the program's success since 1950.

Chapter 8, "White Terror," probes the deadly world of political bandits who steal to finance private wars against society.

Chapter 9, "Armed and Dangerous," presents America's most deadly bandits since the 1930s and examines how their violent crimes have forced police to change their tactics.

Chapter 10, "Prevention and Investigation," describes methods used to prevent and solve bank robberies through the ages, with emphasis on modern techniques.

Although crime doesn't pay, bank robbers keep trying to disprove that theory—and police keep working to frustrate their larcenous plans.

Blood and Money

A cold wind carried the threat of snow along the streets of Liberty, Missouri, on the afternoon of February 13, 1866. Liberty's citizens remained indoors wherever possible, few of them noticing the band of young men who rode into town at 2 p.m. Later, eyewitnesses could not agree if there had been 10 horsemen or 14.

The riders stopped and dismounted outside Liberty's bank. Most remained in the street with their horses, while two went inside. The strangers found cashier Greenup Bird and his son William warming their hands at the bank's small wood stove. The Birds glanced up, expecting customers—and froze as they saw pistols pointed at their faces.

One gunman produced a canvas sack and told the Birds to fill it with cash. His partner stepped into the open vault and found a tin box filled with U.S. government bonds, adding that to their loot. When the bag was full, the outlaws shoved both Birds inside the vault and slammed the door—forgetting to lock it in their hurry.

As the gunmen ran to join their friends outside, the Birds escaped and shouted through a window that the bank was being robbed. Two young men passing by, George Wymore and S.H. Holmes, heard the shouts but had no time to act. The robbers saw Wymore and Holmes and fired their pistols at close range.

One bullet struck and killed George Wymore where he stood. Another tore through Holmes's coat, but he escaped into a nearby shop, unharmed. The gang, meanwhile, rode eastward out of Liberty, some of the bandits whooping high-pitched rebel yells.

Greenup Bird told Sheriff James Jones that the thieves had stolen $15,000 in cash and $45,000 in bonds—a haul worth $600,000 at modern exchange rates. Gang leaders Franklin ("Frank") James (1843–1915) and Thomas Coleman ("Cole") Younger (1844–1916) divided the bonds, while their companions split the currency.

Cole Younger

Bob Younger (rear)

Jesse James

Frank James

Jesse James, Frank James, and the Younger brothers. *Corbis*

Another member of the gang, unrecognized by witnesses, was 18-year-old Jesse Woodson James (1847–1882).

DARK DAYS, DARK DEEDS

America's first daylight bank robbers were not born outlaws. They were natives of Missouri—a state later nicknamed the "Mother of Bandits"—whose simple lives as farmers were disrupted by the curse of slavery and the Civil War. Some say the James and Younger boys were forced by circumstance into a life of crime, while others note that thousands of the outlaws' fellow citizens survived the same hard times and managed to obey the law.

In 1856, five years before 11 southern states seceded from the Union to form a rival country, Congress created the Kansas Territory on the northern border of Missouri. Residents of this area could decide for themselves if slavery would be permitted in their future state. Both sides—slavers and abolitionists—hoped that the final vote would go their way. Some members of each camp engaged in terrorism, spreading violence through the territory. "Bleeding Kansas," as the area was dubbed at the time, gave America a gruesome preview of the coming War Between the States (the American Civil War).

While most combatants in that war were members of regular armed forces, a minority belonged to private guerrilla bands that answered to no authority. Anti-slavery gunmen called "Jayhawkers" or "Red Legs" staged raids in Missouri, robbing and murdering those they suspected of supporting the Confederate rebellion. Missourians retaliated in kind with a force led by William Quantrill (1837–1865), a deranged criminal who tortured animals in childhood and committed his first murder while still a teenager.

In August 1863 Quantrill's raiders invaded Kansas and burned the town of Lawrence, murdering more than 150 unarmed residents in the process. Frank James and Cole Younger both joined in that raid, which provoked a furious reaction from President Abraham Lincoln. To prevent another Lawrence raid, Lincoln issued General Order No. 11, forcibly evacuating 20,000 persons from four Missouri counties bordering Kansas. Soldiers and Jayhawkers drove those people from their homes, leaving a bitter legacy that would endure for years to come.

Jesse James, at age 15, had missed the Lawrence massacre, but he joined Quantrill's band in 1864 and reportedly killed eight men on September 27 during a similar raid on Centralia, Missouri. By war's end, the James and Younger brothers were battle-hardened veterans with bloody hands, accustomed to looting towns and robbing trains.

The sudden shift to peace in April 1865 brought soldiers and guerrillas home to farms neglected or destroyed during the war. Some found it difficult to start anew, while others missed the thrills of wartime—stealing, killing, running for their lives—and saw no reason why the "good times" had to end. By autumn 1865 the James brothers and Cole Younger (with brothers Bob and Jim) had organized a gang of Quantrill veterans with robbery in mind.

At Liberty, in February 1866, the gang made history.

THE OUTLAW TRAIL

The James-Younger gang's second outing—at Lexington, Missouri, on October 30, 1866—proved less impressive than the first. They demanded $100,000 from cashiers at the banking house of Alexander Mitchell & Co., but the vault held a mere $2,000. Still, the raid was a success of sorts because the gang pulled it off without killing anyone. Later, four gang members posing as innocent cowboys joined the sheriff's posse, leading it astray.

A full-scale battle erupted on May 23, 1867, when the gang robbed another bank in Richmond, Missouri. Townspeople fired on the bandits, who fought back with pistols and rifles, killing Mayor John Shaw, jailer William Griffin, and Griffin's 15-year-old son. The gang's take for the holdup was $3,500.

More violence followed the Richmond holdup. A posse tracked gang member Payne Jones to a house near Independence, but Jones escaped after killing a deputy and a girl who led the posse to his hideout. Vigilantes caught another gang member, Dick Burns, and hanged him near Richmond, without a trial. Two other members of the gang, Tom Little and Andy McGuire, were lynched by other mobs before the trail went cold.

On May 20, 1868, Jesse James and Cole Younger stole $14,000 from a bank in Russellville, Kentucky, pistol-whipping a cashier and wounding one bystander outside. That holdup launched a manhunt by agents of the Pinkerton Detective Agency, who captured gang member George Shepherd and saw him sentenced to two years in prison.

Eighteen months passed before the gang struck again, killing bank cashier John Sheets in Gallatin, Missouri, for a mere $700 on December 7, 1869. That disappointing raid produced another lull, broken in June 1871, when the gang stole $10,000 from the Ocobock Brothers' Bank in Corydon, Iowa.

On April 29, 1872, the James and Younger brothers stole a paltry $200 from the Bank of Columbia, Missouri, murdering cashier R.A.C. Martin when he refused to open the safe. Five months later, on September 26, the gang took $10,000 from a bank messenger at the Kansas City fairgrounds, wounding a 10-year-old girl with random gunfire. Another bank holdup—in Ste. Genevieve, Missouri, on May 23, 1873—netted $4,000.

THE PINKERTON WAR

After Ste. Genevieve, the gang returned to its wartime hobby of train-robbing. They uprooted railroad tracks outside Adair, Iowa, on July 21, 1873. This action wrecked an express train, killing its engineer, and the gang escaped with $26,000.

On January 15, 1874, seven gang members robbed a second train at Gad's Hill, Missouri. Before fleeing with an estimated $22,000 in cash, Jesse James delivered his own press release on the holdup, calling it "the most daring on record."

Missouri's governor offered $2,000 for the capture of each James-Younger gang member, while the U.S. Post Office added another $5,000. Pinkerton agents scoured the Missouri countryside, but their luck was bad. Gang members murdered detective James Whicher on March 15 and then killed two more agents—Louis Lull and James Wright—the next day. Lull and Wright went down fighting, killing John Younger (1851–1874) before they were slain.

Pinkerton agents retaliated on January 26, 1875, tossing a bomb into the James family home outside Kearney, Missouri. Zerelda Samuel (1825–1911), mother of Frank and Jesse James, lost an arm in the explosion, while her youngest son was killed. Frank and Jesse got revenge on April 12, killing a neighbor who cooperated with the Pinkertons.

The gang's period of mourning ended on December 13, 1875, when they captured the railroad station at Muncie, Kansas, and stole $60,000 from an incoming train. Seven months later, on

July 7, 1876, the outlaws bagged $15,000 from another train near Otterville, Missouri.

NORTHFIELD

Most outlaws dream of a "score" big enough to let them retire in luxury. Jesse James planned to achieve that goal with a holdup far outside the gang's normal range, in Northfield, Minnesota. Cole Younger disliked the idea, but finally agreed to join the raid against his better judgment.

At 1 p.m. on September 7, 1876, eight bandits approached the First National Bank of Northfield. Their number included Frank and Jesse James; Cole, Bob (1853–1889) and Jim Younger (1848–1902); Bill Chadwell (d. 1876); Clell Miller (1850–1876); and Charlie Pitts (d. 1876). Jesse entered the bank with Pitts and Bob Younger, leaving the rest outside to watch for any trouble.

Inside, the plan immediately fell apart. Cashier J.L. Heywood refused to open the vault, despite threats and a beating, while teller A.E. Bunker escaped from the bank. Bob Younger shot Bunker, but Bunker kept running and raised the alarm. Heywood whipped out a pistol, but Jesse James killed him before he could fire.

On the street, Northfield residents poured from their houses and shops, firing a storm of bullets at the outlaws. Chadwell and Miller died in the shootout, along with townsman Nicholas Gustavson. The other six bandits all suffered painful wounds as they rode out of town empty-handed. Behind them, posses swiftly organized, encouraged by reward offers of $2,200 for the capture of any gang member, dead or alive.

Four days later the gang fought manhunters again near Shieldsville, Minnesota, and then split up. Frank and Jesse left Charlie Pitts with the wounded Youngers. After repeated gunfights and near misses, the James brothers reached the Dakota Territory and escaped. Pitts and the Youngers made their last stand on a farm near Madelia, on September 21. The gunfight proved fatal for Pitts, but the Youngers survived—Cole and Jim with 11 wounds each. At trial, all three were convicted and received 25-year prison terms. Bob succumbed to tuberculosis in prison in 1889, but his brothers survived to be paroled in 1899.

⚲ TRUE LIFE CSI

Jesse James was so popular in some areas that many people refused to believe he was killed in 1882. Rumors spread that Jesse had faked his own death and escaped to Texas, where he lived on as "J. Frank Dalton" until 1951. In July 1995, DNA from surviving members of the James family was compared to that of the corpse in Jesse's grave and confirmed his identity, but some skeptics remained unconvinced. Finally, authorities tried to exhume Frank Dalton in May 2000, but a mix-up in headstones produced the wrong body—that of William Holland, deceased in 1927. Dalton's corpse is still missing, and for some, the mystery of Jesse James endures.

A forensic anthropologist excavates the grave of J. Frank Dalton, who until his death in 1951 claimed that he was really Jesse James and had faked his death 69 years earlier. Dalton's body was not found in the grave and is still missing. *Reuters/ Corbis*

BETRAYED

The Northfield disaster should have discouraged Frank and Jesse James from further crimes, but they joined "Big Nose" George Parrott's (1864–1900) gang to rob a Wyoming train in August 1878. That raid was another fiasco, leaving two civilians dead while the bandits fled empty-handed.

A new James gang, including Clell Miller's brother Ed (c. 1856–1881), resumed bank-robbing at Glendale, Missouri, in October 1879. The crew robbed an Alabama stagecoach in March 1881, then looted a Riverton, Iowa, bank four months later. Five days after that, they robbed a train at Winston, Missouri, and murdered one passenger. Their final train holdup occurred at Blue Cut, Missouri, on September 7, 1881.

By that time, Jesse James had a $10,000 price on his head and he trusted no one, murdering Ed Miller out of fear that Miller might betray him. He was nearly right, but chose the wrong target. Miller was innocent, but another of James's "friends"—Bob Ford (1861–1892)—was plotting against Jesse with his brother Charlie (1857–1884) to collect the payoff.

On April 3, 1882, Jesse welcomed the Ford brothers to his home in St. Joseph, Missouri. When his back was turned, Bob shot him at close range, killing the famous outlaw instantly. Brother Frank surrendered on October 5, 1882, and stood trial for robbery. In yet another shocking twist, jurors acquitted him after James's lawyer mounted a strong defense and discredited the state's star witness, allowing Frank to leave court a free man.

Manhunters

The bandits come in shouting, as if furious, aiming their weapons at the small bank's frightened clerks and customers. They warn against alarms, with threats of death for anyone who disobeys. One of them raids the bank's vault, while another moves behind the cashiers' cages, scooping loot into a bag.

In minutes the outlaws are finished, racing for the exit. This is where the greatest danger lies. If any passerby has seen them, if silent alarms have summoned the police, they may emerge into a storm of gunfire. Or the brief adventure into crime may make them rich. But if they live, they will be hunted. That is guaranteed.

PRIVATE POLICE

Bank robbery was not a federal crime during the first 144 years of United States history. Outlaws could rob a bank, train, or stage-coach in one state and flee to another, where they were safe from arrest. Often, local sheriffs would not chase a gang outside their own counties. As a result, many bandits escaped punishment for their crimes.

To remedy that situation, banks and railroads hired private detectives who could chase outlaws across state lines, or even into foreign countries. Since the private officers were not employed by any government, and only got their pay if they succeeded, they sometimes relied on methods police were not allowed to use. Some were accused of murder, as when Pinkerton detectives bombed the home of Jesse James's mother in Missouri (Chapter 1).

Allan Pinkerton (1819–1884) founded his detective agency in Chicago in 1850. Over the next 60 years Pinkerton agents chased bank and train robbers, guarded President Abraham Lincoln, spied on rebels during the Civil War, infiltrated terrorist groups, and waged violent conflicts against early labor unions. While some historians praise the Pinkertons for bringing law and order to the wild frontier, others—including some former detectives—claimed they were little more than thugs.

Texas cowboy Charles Siringo (1855–1928) joined the Pinkerton Agency in 1886 and worked on some of its most famous cases. In 1912, five years after retiring, Siringo published a memoir titled *Pinkerton's Cowboy Detective.* His stories proved so controversial that Pinkerton lawyers sued him, forcing Siringo to change the book's title to *A Cowboy Detective* and delete negative comments about the agency.

Meanwhile, the Gold Rush of 1849 sparked a new crime wave in California, where hundreds of bandits robbed miners and gold shipments. In 1852 Henry Wells (1805–1878) and William Fargo (1818–1881) started the Wells Fargo banking and express company to protect gold bullion and anything else their customers wanted to transport. By 1866 Wells Fargo coaches monopolized stage lines west of the Mississippi River, remaining in service until 1918.

Wells Fargo also guarded railroad shipments, losing its first to a Nevada gang in 1870. More robberies of coaches and trains followed, but guards like famous frontier lawman Wyatt Earp (1848–1929) made life risky for bandits. Between 1870 and 1884, Wells Fargo reported 347 gold coach holdups. During the same years, 226 bandits were convicted, most captured by Wells Fargo's private detectives and Native American trackers.

One bandit who nearly got away was soft-spoken outlaw Charles Boles (1829–1917), alias "Black Bart." Bolles robbed 26 coaches between 1875 and 1883, often leaving humorous poems with his victims. At his last holdup, Bolles dropped a handkerchief bearing a San Francisco laundry mark. Wells Fargo detectives used it to identify him, trace him, and arrest him. Boles received a six-year prison term. He was released in January 1888 and moved to New York City, where he lived until he died.

ROUGH JUSTICE

Before Pinkerton agents tackled the James-Younger gang in Missouri, they hunted Indiana's train-robbing Reno brothers. That campaign began in 1866 and lasted nearly two years, spanning several states and parts of Canada. Detective Dick Winscott infiltrated the Reno gang in early 1868, luring John Reno (1838–1895) to Cincinnati, Ohio, where Allan Pinkerton arrested him and delivered him to Missouri authorities.

Meanwhile, Frank Reno (1837–1868) led the gang in John's absence, robbing trains, post offices, and other targets across the Midwest. Pinkerton agents staged a series of raids in July 1868, arresting Frank, Simeon (1843–1868), and William Reno (1848–1868), along with nine other gang members. Most would never stand trial, as Indiana lynch mobs hanged three defendants at Seymour on July 24, and four more at New Albany on December 7, 1868.

Allan Pinkerton first condemned the mob violence, but later changed his mind, telling reporters, "The only way to pursue [outlaws] as I see it is to treat them as the Renos were treated in Seymour, Indiana."[1]

Missouri native Tom Horn (1860–1903) killed at least 17 men while working as a Pinkerton detective in the 1880s. On resigning, Horn claimed he had lost his taste for killing. However, he was soon hired out as a "stock detective," shooting suspected cattle thieves for wealthy ranchers in Colorado and Wyoming.

In 1903 Horn was charged with accidentally killing a teenage boy while stalking the boy's father. Pinkerton detective Joe LeFors (1865–1940) got a confession from Horn—some say by feeding him whiskey and twisting his words. True or not, the confession sent Horn to the gallows on November 20, 1903.

BROTHERS IN CRIME

The Dalton brothers—Grattan (1861–1892), Robert (1869–1892), and Emmett (1871–1937)—were cousins of the Younger boys who rode with Frank and Jesse James. Unlike the Youngers, the Daltons first served as lawmen in California and then turned to crime in 1890, fleeing back to their native Missouri the following year. There, they organized a deadly gang that robbed banks and trains in Kansas, Missouri, and Oklahoma.

Those crimes soon put Wells Fargo agents, led by detective Fred Dodge (1854–1938), on the Daltons' trail. Dodge and U.S. Marshal Henry "Heck" Thomas (1850–1912) organized a special "Dalton posse" in May 1891, trailing the gang from one crime scene to another over the next 17 months. The lawmen were always one step behind their targets. Dodge hired an ex-convict to infiltrate the gang, but the Daltons rejected him, saying they had enough gunmen already.

That judgment was proved wrong on October 5, 1892, when the gang tried to rob two banks at once in Coffeyville, Kansas. The Daltons brought three extra men on the raid, but one—Bill Doolin—fell behind when his horse went lame.

Leaving their horses tied in an alley, the raiders split up and moved toward their targets. They bagged $11,000 at one bank and $23,000 at another, but townspeople saw the holdups in progress and rushed for their guns. In the battle that followed, four bandits and four locals died. Of the outlaws, only Emmett Dalton lived, with 23 wounds. All the loot was recovered, except for one $20 bill that vanished without explanation.

Emmett Dalton received a life prison term, serving 14 and a half years before he was pardoned. He died in Los Angeles on July 13, 1937, after seeing his memoirs produced as a Hollywood movie.

Fred Dodge tracked other bandits in the West before retiring in 1918. Wells Fargo paid Heck Thomas $1,500 for his role in the Dalton manhunt, and he moved on to track other "game"—including a survivor of the Dalton gang.

A BANDIT KING

Bill Doolin (1858–1896) missed the Coffeyville massacre and soon organized his own gang, picking up where the Daltons left off. In fact, one of his gunmen *was* a Dalton, brother William (1866–1894). During the four years after Coffeyville, Doolin earned the title "King of the Oklahoma Bandits," leading raids on banks, trains, and stagecoaches across three states.

Wells Fargo agents tracked the Doolin gang, as did U.S. Marshals Heck Thomas, Chris Madsen (1891–1911), and Bill Tilghman (1854–1924). Thirteen marshals faced the gang at Ingalls, Oklahoma, in September 1893, but the shootout ended with three lawmen and two bystanders dead, while all but one of Doolin's outlaws escaped.

The manhunters had better luck after that, killing William Dalton in 1894 and three more gang members in 1895. Tilghman arrested Doolin in January 1896, but Doolin escaped from jail six

ONE WHO GOT AWAY

While Wells Fargo pursued most outlaws without mercy, one famous bandit negotiated a profitable deal with the agency. On April 9, 1913, gunmen led by Francisco "Pancho" Villa (1878–1923) robbed a train in Chihuahua, Mexico, escaping with 122 silver bars

(continues)

General Francisco "Pancho" Villa. *Hulton-Deutsch Collection/ Corbis*

(continued)

valued at $160,000. The robbery was never publicized, a strange fact finally explained in 1999, when librarian Walter Brem found a stash of old letters at the University of California in Berkeley.

The letters, written by Wells Fargo officers in Texas, show that Villa made a deal to sell the silver back to the express company for $50,000. In fact, he returned only 93 of the bars, claiming that his men stole the other 29. Wells Fargo kept the holdup secret, fearing that other rebel groups would follow Villa's example.

While Wells Fargo never punished Pancho Villa, his luck ran out 10 years later. Villa retired from rebel activity in 1920, but his enemies still held grudges. Unknown assassins ambushed Villa's car and killed him at Parral, Chihuahua, on July 23, 1923. Three years later, grave robbers stole Villa's head. It has never been found.

months later. Finally, Heck Thomas traced Doolin to a friend's Oklahoma farm and killed him there on August 25, 1896.

THE WILD BUNCH

America's last major Wild West gang rode and robbed across six states between 1896 and 1903, led by Robert LeRoy Parker (1866–1937), alias Butch Cassidy. Other notorious members included "Sundance Kid" Harry Longabaugh (1867–c. 1908), Ben "the Tall Texan" Kilpatrick (1874–1912), and Harvey "Kid Curry" Logan (1865–1904).

Today, we know Cassidy's gang as the Wild Bunch, a term used for the first time in a 1902 Pinkerton memo to the American Bankers Association. Reporters loved the nickname, but by the time it made headlines, the gang was nearly finished.

While most of the Wild Bunch's robberies produced average hauls (one in 1897 scored only $123), the gang also staged some impressive holdups. In June 1899, Cassidy and three others stole $30,000 from a train in Wyoming. Fifteen months later, Butch and four friends stole $32,640 from a Nevada bank.

The Pinkerton National Detective Agency's wanted poster for the Wild Bunch. *Bettmann/Corbis*

It is no surprise, then, that bankers and railroad companies hired Pinkerton agents to stop the Wild Bunch. Detectives Joe LeFors and Charles Siringo spent months hunting Cassidy, finally spooking Butch so badly that he fled with Longabaugh to South America in 1901.

What happened after that remains unclear. Officially, Butch and Sundance were cornered and killed by Bolivian soldiers in 1908. The story should end there, but several sources (including Cassidy's sister) claimed that both men returned from South America and lived until the 1930s. So far, no DNA tests have confirmed these stories.

A TRADITION CONTINUES

Wells Fargo no longer hunts bandits, but it still suffers robberies. As one of America's major banking companies, it remains a target for stickup artists nationwide. Some major holdups in modern times include

- *1969, New York:* Three gunmen took $1.4 million in racetrack receipts from a Wells Fargo armored truck.
- *1978, New York:* Bandits hit another armored truck while the guards ate lunch. Estimates of their take range from $1 million to $3 million.
- *1983, Tennessee*: Thieves stole $6.5 million from a Wells Fargo office in Memphis. Police recovered $3.2 million.
- *1983, Connecticut:* Puerto Rican nationalists, including Wells Fargo guard Victor Gerena, stole $7.1 million from a company vault. Four bandits were caught. Gerena remains on the FBI's Most Wanted list.
- *1985, New York City:* Three gunmen took $8 million from a Wells Fargo vault, but were soon captured.
- *1997, Florida:* Bandits set a new record, stealing $18.8 million from a company vault in Jacksonville. All but $200,000 was recovered.

Wells Fargo company leaders continue their war against thieves indirectly, through the Wells Fargo Bank Robbery Reward Program, launched in 1991. By December 2000, the program had paid 131 rewards totaling $638,000 to persons whose information helped convict 187 bank robbers.

Lawless Years

December 16, 1932: a relatively quiet afternoon in St. Paul, Minnesota. The 10 employees on duty at the Third Northwestern National Bank outnumber their six customers. At first, they barely notice the four men who enter together—until three of the newcomers draw pistols and the fourth raises a Thompson submachine gun.

The bank tellers cooperate, helping the bandits load their satchels with $20,000 in cash and $10,000 in securities (documents representing a monetary value). Unseen, one bank employee trips a silent alarm that rings at police headquarters. A police dispatcher orders patrolmen Ira Evans and Leo Gorski to investigate.

Evans and Gorski arrive as the bandits emerge from the bank. The machine-gunner spots them and opens fire, striking Evans with 20 bullets and Gorski with five. Both officers are dead before they hit the sidewalk.

The bandits flee, stopping to switch their getaway cars at nearby Como Park. A passerby, Alex Erickson, glances in their direction, then drops with a slug in his brain. The killers disappear without a trace. Another year will pass before FBI agents identify them as members of the deadly Barker-Karpis gang, all of whom would eventually be labeled "public enemies" and arrested or killed.

Throughout history, America has suffered unusual crime waves linked to events such as wars and depressions. One such era, marked by many violent robberies, began soon after World War I and lasted through the Great Depression of the 1930s. Historians attribute the sudden rise of bandit gangs in 1919–33 to various factors. Restless young soldiers wanted more action. Prohibition—the national ban on alcohol—created gangs of bootleggers nationwide after 1920. American farms faced financial collapse in the otherwise prosperous 1920s. The stock market crash of 1929 left millions jobless, while banks foreclosed on their homes.

Whatever the cause, it seemed that suddenly, bandits were everywhere. Gangs overran Oklahoma and Texas. New York City reported 11 holdups in one day (April 7, 1919). Baltimore suffered 100 robberies in November and December 1920. During the same two months, the National Jewelers Board of Trade reported thefts totaling $359,000.

At this point in United States history, something was wrong, and quickly getting worse.

BAD COMPANY

Oklahoma's Indian Territory sheltered outlaws for 70 years before statehood imposed new laws in 1907. The James-Younger gang hid out there, along with the Daltons, Bill Doolin, and countless others. Some had been born there and thus trusted family and friends to hide them between holdups. By 1900 the Cookson Hills, in northeastern Oklahoma, were a notorious refuge for bandits.

Beginning in 1914 Oklahoma suffered an unprecedented wave of bank robberies. Authorities blamed most of them on Henry Starr (1873–1921), a homegrown outlaw who started bootlegging at age 16 and robbed his first bank at 19. Soon afterward, he killed a U.S. Marshal and was twice condemned to hang, but his sentence was reduced on appeal to 25 years.

Starr was released in 1905 and stayed clean until 1908, when he resumed raiding with a new gang. In 1909 Starr received a 25-year sentence for robbery, but publication of his thrilling memoirs in 1913 persuaded Oklahoma's governor to free him—just in time for the state's new crime wave.

In March 1915 Starr repeated the Daltons' mistake, trying to rob two banks at once. Wounded and captured, he received another 25-year sentence, but was once again released in 1919. Starr married and starred in a film about his last bank job, but the straight life quickly paled. In February 1921, Starr suffered fatal wounds during his 25th known robbery, in Harrison, Arkansas.

The next name in criminal headlines was that of Henry Wells (1881–1963), who robbed at least a dozen banks before police caught him in 1916. Wells received a 10-year sentence and soon met outlaw

Portrait of Henry Starr, notorious bank robber. *Bettmann/Corbis*

Ethan "Al" Spencer (1893–1923) in prison. Spencer was a veteran of Henry Starr's gang, and he soon befriended Wells.

Wells was paroled, while Spencer escaped from prison in January 1922. Together, they formed a new gang and robbed 42 banks in the next 20 months. Most were small scores. The gang's greatest haul was $20,000 stolen from a train near Okesa, Oklahoma, on August 23, 1923. Three weeks later, police killed Spencer in a shootout at Bartlesville. Wells served more prison time and then quit the bank-robbing game and lived peacefully to age 82.

Next up on Oklahoma's hit parade was Matthew Kimes (1906–1945), who teamed with brother George (1904–1976) and survivors of the Spencer gang to rob four banks in the summer of 1926. Police caught the Kimes brothers in August, convicting George of robbery and Matthew of killing a deputy sheriff.

Gang members rescued Matt Kimes from jail in November 1926, and three more bank holdups followed in May 1927. Officers recaptured Kimes a month later. He spent 18 years in prison before his next escape, in November 1945. Two weeks later, while police still searched for him, Kimes was struck and killed by a truck in Little Rock, Arkansas.

Surviving members of the Spencer and Kimes gangs carried on Oklahoma's outlaw tradition, becoming some of America's most notorious bandits in the 1930s. Frank "Jelly" Nash (1887–1933) logged his first arrest at age 21 and learned nothing from the experience, chalking up multiple convictions for robbery and murder over the next 12 years. In 1924 he received a 25-year prison term for helping Al Spencer rob the Okesa mail train in August 1923, but Nash escaped in time to play a central role in one of gangland's most explosive episodes (see Chapter 4).

The Barker brothers—Herman (1893–1927), Lloyd (1896–1949), Arthur (1899–1939), and Fred (1902–1935)—also learned their trade with Spencer and Nash. Fred and Arthur, with comrade Alvin Karpis (1908–1979), became the most successful bank robbers and kidnappers of the Great Depression, though none could finally outwit J. Edgar Hoover's FBI, and all were eventually caught.

THE BARON AND THE DEAN

While Oklahoma's badmen relied on family and friends to hide them, bandits in the Midwest practiced "scientific" robbery. Two leaders in the field were Hermann "Baron" Lamm and Harvey Bailey, dubbed the "Dean of Bank Robbers."

⚲ THE NEWTON BOYS

One of the lawless era's most successful outlaw gangs, if not the most notorious, included the four Newton brothers—Jess (1887–1960), Willis (1889–1979), William or "Doc" (1891–1974), and Joe (1901–89)—with various accomplices. The Newtons suffered several scrapes with the law after 1907, serving jail time on multiple charges, then turned to armed robbery in 1914. Over the next 14 years their crimes ranged from Texas to Canada, where they robbed 80-odd banks and six trains, climaxing their career with the biggest train robbery in American history.

That holdup occurred at Rondout, Illinois, on June 12, 1924. William Fahy, a U.S. postal inspector, sold the gang information that permitted them to steal $3 million from the Chicago, Milwaukee, and St. Paul mail train. The holdup went smoothly until an accomplice accidentally shot Doc Newton, nearly killing him.

Federal agents soon arrested Fahy and identified the bandits. While Fahy received a 25-year sentence, the Newtons exchanged their loot for more lenient punishment. Doc served six years, Willis four years and two months, Joe one year, and Jess nine months.

Paroled in the midst of Prohibition, Willis Newton turned bootlegger. Treasury agents soon jailed him for smuggling whiskey, and Texas authorities charged Willis and Joe for a recent bank holdup. Both denied involvement in the crime, but they received 20-year sentences. Joe served 10 years, while Willis served seven and a half.

Doc Newton came out of retirement at age 77 to rob another Texas bank in 1968. Shot and wounded at the scene, he spent several months in jail. He was released to a nursing home where he later died of lung cancer. Willis and Joe participated in a documentary film about their careers as outlaws, which was filmed in 1976, but neither lived to see Hollywood's romanticized version of their story, *The Newton Boys*, released in 1998, starring Matthew McConaughey as Willis, Skeet Ulrich as Joe, Ethan Hawke as Jess, and Vincent D'Onofrio as Doc Newton.

Lamm (1890–1930) was born in Germany and planned a military career, but the army dismissed him for cheating at cards. He immigrated to America and turned to crime, serving a prison term in Utah for armed robbery in 1917. Thereafter, Lamm applied his military training to bank holdups, planning each raid like an army campaign.

Lamm's plan had three phases. First, he studied each bank and drew detailed floor plans. Next, he conducted rehearsals, using models of the target. Finally, Lamm mapped and timed escape routes, using fast cars and skilled drivers.

Between 1917 and 1930, Lamm robbed many banks across the country, while teaching his method to younger outlaws. His luck ran out in December 1930 when his getaway car broke down after a holdup in Clinton, Indiana. Police trapped Lamm and three companions in a cornfield, killing Lamm in the battle that followed.

Harvey Bailey (1887–1979) followed honest trades until 1920, when Prohibition offered easy money for bootleggers. Bailey soon switched to burglarizing banks after hours, and then turned to daylight robbery in 1922. His first known holdup, in Ohio, scored $265,000. Bailey was also suspected, but never charged, in the $200,000 Denver Mint robbery of December 1922.

After those large scores, Bailey "went straight," or gave up his life of crime, for four years, returning to robbery full time in 1926. Over the next five years, Bailey's gang robbed at least 12 banks in six states, stealing $4.2 million. In July 1932 FBI agents found Bailey golfing in St. Louis with two fugitives from federal prison. In his pocket, they found bank loot from a Kansas robbery, and Bailey got a prison term of 10 to 50 years.

Instead of serving his time, Bailey escaped with 10 other convicts in May 1933, forming another gang that robbed three banks during July and August. Bailey's bad luck with friends continued, however. When George "Machine Gun" Kelly paid a debt to Bailey, he used money from a recent ransom kidnapping. FBI agents nabbed Bailey on August 12, matched serial numbers from the ransom bills, and convicted Bailey of a crime he did not commit.

This time, Bailey stayed in prison, serving 28 years of a life sentence before his release in 1961. Kansas took him back to serve more time on the 1932 robbery charge, releasing Bailey in 1965, at age 68.

Officers guard Harvey Bailey (second from right). Bailey was being held for the kidnapping of Charles F. Urschel, a crime he did not commit. *Bettmann/Corbis*

FIGHTING BACK

Americans reacted to the great crime wave of the early twentieth century in different ways, though none proved truly effective. As in our own time, the plans included civilian participation in crime fighting, use of new technology, financial rewards for the capture of bandits, and harsh punishment for those arrested.

Private vigilance committees played a large role in Old West crime fighting, and their revival seemed to be a quick fix during 1920–1933. The only vigilante victory occurred at Boley, Oklahoma, where citizens killed two bank robbers and captured a third on November 23, 1932. Boley's bank president also died in that shootout.

New police technology in the period between 1919 and 1933 consisted mainly of machine guns, faster vehicles, and radio dispatch systems. Chicago and Detroit pioneered the use of police radios, prompting 51 other cities to follow by 1929. The U.S. Post Office bought 3,000 armored cars in 1924 to stop mail robberies. The sheriff of Lake County, Indiana, got an airplane to chase bandits but never used it. Chicago merchants demanded shotguns and electric sirens for their stores, while the local banker's association planned underground tunnels to protect cash shipments.

Cash rewards have been offered throughout history for the capture of outlaws. In the 1920s, however, they often seemed more like a license to kill. The Chicago Bankers Association offered $2,500 for each robber slain, while the Detroit Clearing House Association raised it to $5,000. The Texas Bankers Association matched that figure for dead bandits, adding "not one cent for live ones."[1] Milwaukee's Clearing House was less bloodthirsty, offering $2,500 for dead outlaws and $1,000 for those caught alive.

Harsh punishment is a common public response to sensational crimes. During 1919 to 1933, three states passed laws to permit public whipping of robbers, with Delaware adding a 20-year jail term to its 40 lashes. The citizens of Woodlynne, New Jersey, preferred tar and feathers. Three other states imposed a death sentence for robbery. New York doubled its maximum sentence from 20 to 40 years, and New Jersey voted life terms for "highwaymen." Police chiefs in several large cities ordered bandits shot on sight, and Chicago reported 70 "outlaws" killed in 1931 alone.

Those efforts all made headlines, but they did not solve the problem. It would take a national crime war to turn the tide, and even that would only have short-term success.

Gangbusters

Prison breaks were easier to accomplish in 1930 than they are today. Some lockups, like Oklahoma's state prison, granted leaves of absence for convicts to visit their lawyers or families, even to go hunting or fishing. Most inmates returned on schedule, but a few just kept going, right back to their old lives of crime.

Leavenworth Federal Prison in Kansas allowed no such field trips, but during the Great Depression security was often lax. On October 19, 1930, while serving 25 years for mail robbery, inmate Frank Nash (1887–1933) borrowed a book from the prison library and strolled through the gates to freedom.

He fled first to St. Paul, Minnesota, where gangsters on the run were always welcome. There, Nash joined a gang of fugitives from Leavenworth and started robbing banks again. Between April 1931 and April 1933 the gang raided banks in five states, stealing $432,000.

In June 1933 Nash settled with his new bride in Hot Springs, Arkansas, another town that coddled criminals. Although local police ignored Nash, FBI agents spotted him and arrested him on June 16. They put him on a train to Kansas City, where another group of officers would meet them for the drive to Leavenworth. Angry and frightened, Frances Nash phoned Kansas City, seeking someone who could set her husband free.

MURDER IN TOM'S TOWN

Gangsters were not hard to find in Kansas City in the 1930s. Corrupt political boss Thomas Pendergast (1873–1945) ran the city's government with help from mobster John Lazia (1896–1934),

Prison photos of Frank Nash. *Bettmann/Corbis*

hand-picking Democratic candidates who included future U.S. President Harry Truman.

Pendergast's control was so complete that some observers nicknamed Kansas City "Tom's Town." Gambling, illegal saloons, prostitution, and other forms of crime operated without interference from police, while gangsters on the run could always find safe haven for a price.

One criminal who made his home in Tom's Town was Verne Miller (1896–1933), a decorated hero of World War I and former South Dakota sheriff who left office in disgrace after stealing $4,000 in county funds. He served a year in prison for that crime, where he worked as the warden's chauffeur. He then emerged to earn his living as a bank robber and contract killer. Miller spoke to Frances Nash on June 16 and promised her that he would spring Frank from his captors.

Nash and his three escorts reached Kansas City's Union Station at 7 a.m. on June 17, 1933. More FBI agents and local officers were waiting, with two cars, for the 20-mile trip to Leavenworth.

As they approached their cars, several gunmen appeared, shouting for the lawmen to raise their hands. A shot rang out from one FBI car, and the gangsters cut loose with machine guns, riddling both vehicles. When the smoke cleared, four lawmen and Frank Nash lay dead.

The Kansas City massacre shocked America and enraged FBI Director J. Edgar Hoover. Federal agents soon identified Verne Miller as one of the gunmen, but confused eyewitness testimony made the others hard to track. At last, a full year after the murders, Hoover announced that Miller's accomplices were Oklahoma bandit Charles "Pretty Boy" Floyd (1904–1934) and his partner, Adam Richetti (1909–1938).

By that time, Verne Miller was dead, murdered by rival gangsters outside Detroit, Michigan, in November 1923. Floyd and Richetti hid in Buffalo, New York, until October 1934, when they drifted back to the Midwest in search of fresh banks to rob.

Floyd wrecked their car outside East Liverpool, Ohio, on October 19, and police soon located the fugitives. Richetti surrendered after a brief shootout, but Floyd escaped to a nearby farm, where officers cornered and killed him on October 22. With his dying breath, Floyd denied participating in the Kansas City murders.

Adam Richetti also claimed that he was innocent. The only evidence against him was a fingerprint, recovered from a beer bottle at Verne Miller's home, but jurors accepted the print as proof of his guilt. They convicted Richetti of murder in June 1935, and he received a death sentence. On October 7, 1938, he became the first inmate to die in Ohio's new gas chamber.

Controversy still surrounds the FBI's solution to the Kansas City case. One witness to the shootings, a policeman, described a second carload of gunmen firing on Nash and his escorts, but no other shooters were ever identified.

"OPEN" CITIES

Tracking fugitives like Miller, Floyd, and Richetti was hard enough without interference from corrupt police and politicians. Honest manhunters found it even more difficult in so-called open cities, where criminals could find protection for a price.

Scene after the Kansas City Massacre. Frank Nash and four law enforcement officials were killed in a hail of gunfire. *Bettmann/ Corbis*

Tom Pendergast's Kansas City was one such gangster hangout. Two others were Hot Springs, Arkansas (where FBI agents caught Nash), and St. Paul, Minnesota (where Nash joined his last bank-robbing gang).

Hot Springs got its name from natural springs of water heated to 147 degrees by underground seismic action. The springs have drawn millions of tourists since the 1880s, including both the famous and notorious. Well-known visitors to Hot Springs have included Frank and Jesse James, frontier marshal Bat Masterson, various star athletes, and several United States presidents.

The busy tourist industry inspired a sideline of illegal gambling. Lawman Wyatt Earp once became so enraged at his losses in Hot Springs that local police disarmed him and escorted him out of town. New York gangster Owney Madden took over Hot

"DON'T SHOOT, G-MEN!"

Outlaw George "Machine Gun" Kelly (1895–1954) spent four months in college before dropping out in 1917 to drive a taxi. Three years later, Prohibition lured him to the easy life of a bootlegger. Kelly's third arrest for smuggling liquor sent him to Leavenworth in 1928, where he met Frank Nash and other veterans of Al Spencer's bank-robbing gang. The others soon escaped, and Kelly joined them when he was paroled in June 1930.

Over the next two years, Kelly participated in six bank hold-ups, stealing $312,000. In January 1932 he tried a new game, kidnapping an Indiana banker's son and collecting $50,000 ransom. In July 1933, Kelly and comrade Al Bates snatched Oklahoma oilman Charles Urschel, releasing him after nine days in exchange for $200,000.

It was easy money, but Congress had passed the Lindbergh Law since Kelly's first kidnapping. Police and FBI agents soon located the Texas farm, owned by relatives of Kelly's wife, where Urschel had been held. They also nabbed bank-robber Harvey Bailey in the process, but Kelly was not at the farm.

A month later, on September 22, authorities traced him to a rooming house in Memphis, Tennessee. FBI agents later claimed that Kelly cowered before their guns, tearfully begging them, "Don't shoot, G-men! Don't shoot!"

The *G-man* nickname—short for "government man"—made national headlines and sticks to this day, although many FBI agents are now G-*women*.

The legend of Machine Gun Kelly's plea is false, however. Memphis officers arrested Kelly in his room, while raiders from the FBI remained outside the house. And far from pleading with his captors, Kelly seemed relieved. His true words were: "I've been expecting you."[2]

Kelly, wife Katherine, and Al Bates received life prison terms for the Urschel kidnapping. So did Katherine's parents, her brother, and Harvey Bailey (who played no part in the crime). George Kelly died in prison on July 18, 1954. Katherine and her mother were freed five years later, when FBI agents inexplicably refused to furnish an appellate court with files on the case.

Springs' gambling rackets in the early 1930s, welcoming guests who included Chicago's Al Capone and New York Mafia boss Lucky Luciano. Whenever the "heat" (that is, law enforcement) became too intense in their own cities, American gangsters knew they could hide in Hot Springs without fear of arrest.

St. Paul made felons feel most welcome. There, instead of simply hiding outlaws for a price—or warning them when raids could not be avoided—police and politicians sometimes helped gangs plan their future crimes.

Normally, such help required a promise from the gangsters that they would only raid targets outside of St. Paul. In January 1934, however, crooked officials helped members of the Barker-Karpis gang kidnap banker George Bremer from his St. Paul home. After relatives paid $200,000 ransom on February 7, political bosses John McLaughlin and Harry Sawyer got part of the money.

Their greed backfired in January 1935, when federal prosecutors indicted McLaughlin, Sawyer, and 21 others for Bremer's kidnapping. FBI agents killed Fred Barker (1902–1935) and his mother in Florida on January 15, and soon arrested most of the other defendants. McLaughlin got a five-year prison term, while Sawyer was sentenced to life in January 1936. The scandal produced a clean-up in St. Paul.

Alvin Karpis (1907–1979) remained at large until May 1936, when FBI agents captured him in New Orleans. He also received a life term, serving 32 and a half years before his release in January 1969.

WASHINGTON'S WAR ON CRIME

America had tolerated countless holdups, gang wars, and murders since 1920, treating many of the nation's headline-grabbing crimes as free entertainment. Bootleggers quenched the public's thirst in Prohibition, and the victims of their feuds were mostly other criminals. During the Great Depression, few Americans felt any sympathy for bankers who were robbed. Some bandits, like Pretty Boy Floyd, earned public sympathy by burning mortgage papers in the banks they looted.

That sympathy faded between 1932 and 1933, however, after the Kansas City massacre and several high-profile ransom kidnappings. In Washington, D.C., J. Edgar Hoover lobbied Congress for new laws to let his agents pursue the nation's "public enemies."

Step one was the Lindbergh Law, passed by Congress in June 1932, three months after unknown kidnappers snatched the infant son of hero aviator Charles Lindbergh. The law made it a federal crime to carry kidnap victims across state lines. An amendment, added in 1934, permitted execution of kidnappers whose victims suffered any injury.

A year after the Kansas City murders, in June 1934, Congress passed another series of laws greatly expanding the FBI's authority. The new laws made it a federal crime to transport stolen property between states, to rob any bank insured by the U.S. government, to assault or kill federal agents, or to flee across state lines from trial or prison. Furthermore, America's first federal gun-control law placed restrictions on civilian ownership of "gangster weapons" such as machine guns, firearm silencers, and sawed-off shotguns.

Armed with new authority, FBI agents fanned out across the country pursuing bandits and kidnappers, fighting a series of battles with outlaws from Chicago and Ohio to New York and Florida. Agents killed 10 fugitives and lost three of their own to hostile fire, while newspapers covered the action in banner headlines.

Sometimes, a bit of explanation was required, as when agents shot 62-year-old Arizona Barker along with her son Fred, a notorious bank-robber and kidnapper, in January 1935. No evidence exists that Mrs. Barker ever committed a crime, but FBI spokesmen mounted a publicity campaign against her, branding "Ma" Barker as the evil mastermind of the Barker-Karpis gang. That image survives in Hollywood films such as *Ma Barker's Killer Brood* (1960), *Bloody Mama* (1970), and *Public Enemies* (1996), but those who knew her in life held a different view. Gang member Harvey Bailey told reporters, "The old lady couldn't plan breakfast."[1]

Public Enemy No. 1

Half a century passed between Jesse James's death and the emergence of another outlaw with the same notoriety. The new gangland superstar's career was brief—only 14 months versus Jesse's 16 years on the run—but his name became, and still remains, a household word.

No one forgets the story of John Dillinger.

WRONG TURNS

Despite the claims of various historians, John Herbert Dillinger (1903–1934) was not a farm boy who went bad through no fault of his own. He was born in Indianapolis in June 1903, and lost his mother three years later. Dillinger was 12 when his father remarried and moved the family to a farm outside Mooresville. The move came *after* Dillinger's first juvenile arrest.

Dillinger joined the navy in 1923, but he hated discipline and soon deserted. Back in Mooresville, he found work but did not like it. In September 1924, with 31-year-old Edward Singleton, Dillinger beat and robbed a local grocer.

Police caught both thieves, and Dillinger pled guilty on advice from his lawyer. He received a sentence of two to 20 years and served almost nine. Singleton took his chances with a jury and served only two years.

State prison schooled Dillinger for a career in crime. While bitter at his sentence, he found friends inside and learned from them. Veteran bank robbers Harry Pierpont (1902–1934), Charles Makley (1889–1934), Russell Clark (1898–1968), John Hamilton

WANTED

JOHN HERBERT DILLINGER

On June 23, 1934, HOMER S. CUMMINGS, Attorney General of the United States, under the authority vested in him by an Act of Congress approved June 6, 1934, offered a reward of

$10,000.00

for the capture of John Herbert Dillinger or a reward of

$5,000.00

for information leading to the arrest of John Herbert Dillinger.

DESCRIPTION

Age, 32 years; Height, 5 feet 7-1/8 inches;
Weight, 153 pounds; Build, medium; Hair,
medium chestnut; Eyes, grey; Complexion,
medium; Occupation, machinist; Marks and
scars, 1/2 inch scar back left hand, scar
middle upper lip, brown mole between eye-
brows.

All claims to any of the aforesaid rewards and all questions and disputes that may arise as among claimants to the foregoing rewards shall be passed upon by the Attorney General and his decisions shall be final and conclusive. The right is reserved to divide and allocate portions of any of said rewards as between several claimants. No part of the aforesaid rewards shall be paid to any official or employee of the Department of Justice.

If you are in possession of any information concerning the whereabouts of John Herbert Dillinger, communicate immediately by telephone or telegraph collect to the nearest office of the Division of Investigation, United States Department of Justice, the local addresses of which are set forth on the reverse side of this notice.

JOHN EDGAR HOOVER, DIRECTOR,
DIVISION OF INVESTIGATION,
UNITED STATES DEPARTMENT OF JUSTICE,
WASHINGTON, D. C.

June 25, 1934

U.S. Department of Justice wanted poster of infamous bank robber John Dillinger. *Bettmann/Corbis*

(1898–1934), and Homer Van Meter (1906–1934) taught Dillinger everything they knew about holdups. In return, Dillinger promised to help them escape after he was released.

Parole came for Dillinger on May 22, 1933. He robbed a supermarket 18 days later with an Indianapolis gang called the White Caps. More holdups followed, including Dillinger's first bank job on June 10, in Ohio. By early September the gang's take topped $51,000.

Dillinger bought pistols and tossed them over the state prison's wall, but they never reached his friends inside. Next, he smuggled more guns into the prison sewing shop. Pierpont, Makley, Hamilton, Clark, and three other convicts escaped on September 26—but Dillinger was back in jail by then, arrested for bank robbery four days earlier.

On October 12, 1933, Dillinger's pals returned the favor, liberating him from jail in Lima, Ohio. In the process, Pierpont murdered Sheriff Jesse Sarber.

There could be no turning back.

DILLINGER GANG: ROUND ONE

The new gang armed itself with guns and bulletproof vests stolen from small police stations. Over the next three months, the fugitives pulled at least four holdups, stealing some $259,000. Shootouts with police left two more officers dead.

At that point, Indiana State Police commander Matt Leach (1895–1955) hatched a plan to destroy the gang from within. Leach assumed correctly that Harry Pierpont was the new gang's leader, but he publicly called it "the Dillinger gang," hoping to spark Pierpont's jealousy and break up the group. On December 28, the Chicago Crime Commission listed Dillinger as "Public Enemy No. 1," with Pierpont rated second.

The tactic failed. It inflated Dillinger's image, but Pierpont ignored the reports and stuck to the business of crime. In January 1934 the gang vacationed in Arizona, where Tucson's sheriff recognized them from WANTED posters. Dillinger, Pierpont, Makley, and Clark were arrested on January 25. Dillinger faced charges of killing an Indiana policeman, while the rest went back to Ohio for trial in Sheriff Sarber's murder.

ESCAPE!

On March 3, 1934, Dillinger escaped from the heavily guarded jail at Crown Point, Indiana. Most reports claim that he used a hand-carved wooden gun blackened with shoe polish. Some sources claim a real pistol was smuggled into jail by Dillinger's lawyer. One story suggests that Dillinger carved the fake gun after the real weapon failed to arrive.

Whatever the truth, Dillinger took hostages inside the jail, and then armed himself and another inmate with machine guns before stealing the sheriff's car. Dillinger fled to Chicago, thus breaking a federal law that bans driving stolen cars across state lines.

Now he was hunted by the FBI.

In Chicago, Dillinger joined a new gang that included John Hamilton (1899–1934), Homer Van Meter, George "Baby Face" Nelson (1908–1934), Tommy Carroll (1897–1934), and Eddie Green (d. 1934). Three days after Dillinger's escape, the gang stole $49,500 from a bank in Sioux Falls, South Dakota, wounding a policeman in the process. One week later, they bagged $52,344 from another bank in Mason City, Iowa.

Both Dillinger and Hamilton were wounded in the second holdup, but they bounced back quickly. Witnesses blamed the gang for a third bank robbery ($27,000) at Pana, Illinois, on April 19.

After that, they needed a break.

LITTLE BOHEMIA

Emil Wanatka's Little Bohemia Lodge in the woods outside Rhine-lander, Wisconsin, seemed a perfect place for the bandits to hide and relax. Wanatka recognized them, and while the outlaws watched his family closely, Emil's wife still managed to send off a letter, telling Chicago G-men where the gang could be found.

On April 22, 1934, Agent Melvin Purvis (1903–1960) led an FBI strike force to Wisconsin, traveling first by plane, and then by road. One of their cars broke down along the way, forcing several agents to ride on the second car's running boards. Reaching the lodge after dark, some of the G-men stumbled into a barbed-wire fence and alerted Wanatka's watchdogs.

Just then, three innocent customers left the lodge's restaurant. Nervous agents thought they were gangsters and shot all three, killing one. Thus alerted, the bandits fought back and escaped through rear windows in darkness, leaving only their girlfriends behind. Baby Face Nelson, separated from the others, shot three lawmen at a nearby store, killing FBI agent Carter Baum.

Melvin Purvis was embarrassed by the raid's outcome. Long months would pass before he learned that John Hamilton had been killed while running a police roadblock with Dillinger and Van Meter, outside St. Paul, Minnesota.

Furious, J. Edgar Hoover placed agent Samuel Cowley in charge of the manhunt, with orders to wipe out the gang.

NOWHERE TO HIDE

By that time, Eddie Green was already dead, shot by G-men in St. Paul (although he was unarmed) on April 3. Tommy Carroll went next, cut down when he pulled a gun on police in Waterloo, Iowa, on June 7, 1934.

Dillinger robbed his last bank on June 30 in South Bend, Indiana, escaping with $29,890. The gang—including Nelson, Van Meter, John Paul Chase (1901–1973), and two others—killed a policeman as they fled. Some witnesses said that Pretty Boy Floyd was along for the ride, a claim still debated by gangland historians.

The noose was tightening. Attorney General Homer Cummings branded Dillinger America's top public enemy, offering $10,000 for his capture or $5,000 for information leading to his arrest. Authorities now blamed the gang for murdering two Indiana policemen in May 1934, and for wounding two more officers outside Chicago on July 14.

If Dillinger was caught alive, he had a date with the electric chair.

BETRAYED

Anna Sage (1892–1947) had troubles of her own in July 1934. A Romanian immigrant, she faced deportation for running a house of prostitution in Chicago. On July 21 she met with Agents Cowley and Purvis to make a deal. One of her frequent customers was Dillinger, she said. She would betray him for the $5,000 reward, and for the FBI's help to remain in America.

The G-men agreed.

On July 22 Dillinger went to the Biograph Theater with Sage and one of her girls, Polly Hamilton. FBI agents waited outside the theater, surrounding Dillinger when he emerged at 10:35 p.m. Dillinger ran for an alley and died in a hail of bullets. The FBI soon forgot its promise to Sage, and she was deported in 1936.

A view of the scene of John Dillinger's death. Dillinger had attended a movie in the Biograph Theatre on the left when FBI agents closed in on him. He was surrounded when he reached the alley on the right. Agents shot and killed him when he attempted to draw a gun. *Bettmann/Corbis*

THE ROUNDUP

Dillinger's comrades did not last long without him. Police in St. Paul killed Homer Van Meter on August 22. Exactly one month later, Makley and Pierpont tried to escape from Ohio's death row with pistols carved from soap. Guards killed Makley and wounded Pierpont. Pierpont recovered in time to die in the electric chair, on October 17.

On November 27 FBI agents spotted Baby Face Nelson and John Chase in Illinois. After a high-speed chase Nelson stopped near

♀ DEAD OR ALIVE?

Americans hate to let go of their favorite outlaws. Over the past 126 years, rumors have circulated that various badmen—including Jesse James, Billy the Kid, Butch Cassidy, and "Sundance Kid" Harry Longabaugh—faked their own deaths and survived in retirement for decades. The same is said of Dillinger.

Rumors of survival began immediately after his death, when his father refused to identify Dillinger's body. Authorities blamed that lapse on Dillinger's recent plastic surgery performed by an underworld doctor.

In 1963 the *Indianapolis Star* received a letter and photo from a California man who claimed to be Dillinger. When editors ignored the letter, the man wrote to Emil Wanatka Jr. Chicago author Jay Nash later published a book, *Dillinger: Dead or Alive?* (1970), claiming that the man was indeed Dillinger.

According to Nash, Dillinger paid gangsters and corrupt police to find a stand-in for his death scene. They chose one Jimmy Lawrence, who resembled Dillinger, and G-men accidentally killed Lawrence in Dillinger's place. Later, the FBI allegedly buried its mistake to avoid embarrassment. Nash cites the following evidence to prove his case

- Dillinger's autopsy report omits mention of various prominent scars, wounds, and birthmarks.
- The corpse was notably shorter than Dillinger's recorded height.

(continues)

(continued)

- The report lists brown eyes, while Dillinger's were gray.
- The dead man had rheumatic heart disease, never mentioned in Dillinger's medical files from the navy or prison.

Critics replied that Audrey Dillinger identified her brother's body by a scar on one leg, while his gray eyes may have been discolored by a fatal head wound. Dr. Patrick Weeks, formerly of Indiana's state prison, claimed that Dillinger *did* have rheumatic heart disease in 1933, although it was not noted in his file (and it contradicts his lifelong athletic behavior). FBI spokesmen explain the other discrepancies as simple mistakes, insisting that they had matched Dillinger's fingerprints to the Chicago corpse.

Nash did reveal one final mystery, however. Tracing the serial number of Dillinger's supposed pistol, removed from his body in 1933 and displayed for many years at FBI headquarters, Nash proved the gun was manufactured months *after* Dillinger died. Author Joe Pinkston claimed that J. Edgar Hoover gave the original gun to an unnamed Hollywood celebrity as a gift, then replaced it with a later model. Nash, meanwhile, believes that the switch proves Dillinger was shot while unarmed.

Barrington to shoot it out with Agents Sam Cowley and Herman Hollis. He killed both G-men, but died that night from his 17 wounds. Chase was captured one month later in California and received a life sentence for the Illinois murders.

Many friends of Dillinger were also jailed on various charges, mostly for harboring federal fugitives. One, James Probasco, allegedly committed suicide by jumping from the FBI's 19th-floor office in Chicago, five days after Dillinger died. John Chase was paroled over J. Edgar Hoover's objections in October 1966. Russell Clark was released in December 1968 and died four months later.

GONE BUT NOT FORGOTTEN

Ironically, John Dillinger and the publicity surrounding his case helped make the FBI what it is today. Gangbusting G-men became overnight heroes. For many years, Dillinger's photograph adorned targets on the FBI pistol range. Tourists can still view his plaster death mask and personal effects at FBI headquarters in Washington, D.C.

Dillinger is the subject of at least 25 nonfiction books, eight novels, 11 movies, a short story by Stephen King ("The Death of Jack Hamilton," in *Everything's Eventual*) , and an epic poem penned by author Todd Moore. A small group of loyal fans still celebrate July 22 each year as "John Dillinger Day."

Where the Money Is

Modern bank robbers are an endangered species. While thousands rob banks in the United States every year, few display the cunning of Baron Lamm, the flamboyant style of John Dillinger, or the long-term success of Harvey Bailey. And none have criminal careers on par with Willie Sutton (1901–1980).

Between 1926 and 1950, Sutton robbed an estimated 100 banks—even though he spent nearly half of his adult life in prison. He stole an estimated $2 million overall, equivalent to some $20 million at modern exchange rates.

Sutton preferred the name Bill, but police called him Willie. Reporters dubbed him "The Actor" or "Willie the Actor" because of his clever disguises. To prison guards, he was "Slick Willie," the consummate escape artist.

Strangely, although he carried pistols and machine guns on his raids, his victims remembered Sutton as a gentleman. One remarked that living through a Sutton holdup was like going to the movies—except that the usher was armed. Unknown to most of those he robbed, the guns were rarely loaded. Sutton was concerned that someone might get hurt.

After his last arrest, a journalist claimed that Sutton said he robbed banks because "that's where the money is." Shortly before his death, Sutton denied the comment but admitted that he *might* have said it, had anyone bothered to ask. In fact, Sutton said he robbed banks for the thrill of it, feeling more alive in the midst of a holdup than at any other time. The money was just a sweet fringe benefit.

Bank robber Willie Sutton, known as "The Actor" because of his use of disguises, in custody in 1952. *Hulton-Deutsch Collection/Corbis*

TOUGH GUY

William Francis Sutton was born in an Irish neighborhood in Brooklyn, a borough of New York City, on June 30, 1901. He dropped out of school in eighth grade and briefly joined a local street gang, but the petty crimes of juvenile delinquents did not entertain him. Sutton had big dreams. He wanted to become a lawyer and defend his hoodlum friends in court, but law school was expensive and he never held a steady job for more than 18 months.

In 1917 young love propelled him into conflict with police for the first time. Sutton burglarized a jewelry store owned by his girl-friend's father, stealing $16,000 to finance their elopement. Instead of getting married, he was charged with multiple felonies, later bargained down to one count of unlawful entry. Sutton spent a year in reform school, while the rest of his sentence was suspended.

THE BIG TIME

No record exists of Sutton's movements from mid-1918 to July 1921, when authorities indicted him on a double murder charge. Two enemies of Sutton had been shot outside a New York City pool hall, and while Sutton denied playing any part in the killings, he joined a safe-cracking gang and went into hiding.

Police eventually found Sutton and held him for trial. If convicted, he could have faced a date with the electric chair. No one seemed more surprised than Sutton when jurors pronounced him not guilty.

At his next trial, in April 1926, he was convicted of bank burglary, receiving a sentence of five to 10 years in prison. Paroled in August 1929, Sutton joined mobster Dutch Schultz's bootlegging gang. He then left organized crime to launch a new career robbing banks and jewelry stores.

It was during this phase of his life that Sutton earned his reputation as "Willie the Actor." Using costumes and makeup, he disguised himself on various jobs as a policeman, a firefighter, or a Western Union messenger. When not in disguise, Sutton revealed his fashion sense as a stylish dresser with expensive tastes.

While Sutton's raids were not always successful, he never quit trying. On October 10, 1930, he dressed as a messenger to rob a bank in Brooklyn, but a watchman foiled the holdup. Sutton rebounded on October 28, wearing the same disguise to steal gems worth $130,000 from a jeweler's shop on Broadway.

Sutton's luck went sour again in June 1931, when he received a 30-year sentence for bank robbery. Caged at New York's notorious

Sing Sing prison, Sutton soon displayed his skill as an escape artist. He scaled the wall with homemade ladders on December 12, 1932, and formed a new gang to resume his outlaw career.

In February 1933, bystanders interrupted Sutton's robbery of a bank in Philadelphia—an episode during which he was dressed as a postman. Five months later, with two friends and a machine gun, he stole $23,838 from another branch of the same bank in New York. Then, in January 1934, he returned to the Philadelphia branch and bagged another $10,980.

It was a daring move, but costly. Philadelphia police arrested Sutton in February 1934. He received a prison term of 25 to 50 years for his latest holdups. Authorities vowed that Eastern State Prison would hold him.

But they were mistaken.

SLICK WILLIE

At Eastern State, Sutton quickly lived up to another nickname— "Slick Willie." During his first decade behind bars, he made four escape attempts, all foiled by prison guards.

But Sutton never quit trying.

On April 3, 1945, he escaped with 11 other convicts through a tunnel they had dug beneath the walls of Eastern State Prison. It was another bold move, but police recaptured Sutton the same day in Philadelphia. His clever plan was ruined by his need to revisit old haunts.

Tried for the prison break as a fourth-time offender, Sutton was convicted and sentenced to life imprisonment. To no one's great surprise, that sentence only made him more determined to escape. Seeking to frustrate any new attempts, authorities placed Sutton in maximum security at Homesburg's Philadelphia County Prison.

They may as well have handed him the keys.

After nightfall on February 10, 1947, in the midst of a snowstorm, Sutton and two other inmates slipped out of their cells, donned stolen guards' uniforms, and carried two ladders to the outer wall. Searchlights found them halfway up, but Sutton waved and shouted, "It's okay!"

Incredibly, the prison sentries let him go.

Snow covered Sutton's tracks and he escaped.

TOP TEN

Sutton was still at large on January 17, 1950, when unknown thieves stole nearly $3 million from a Brinks vault in Boston (see Chapter 7). Police suspected him of planning or participating in the raid, which seemed to have his style.

They were wrong, but Sutton was soon back in action, joining two other bandits to steal $63,933 from a bank in Queens on March 9, 1950. Witnesses identified Sutton from his mug shots as

♀ SILENCED WITNESS

Most Americans agreed that 24-year-old Arnold Schuster had performed a public service in February 1952, when he recognized Willie Sutton on a subway train and notified police. One television viewer who disagreed was Albert Anastasia, boss of New York City's Mangano (later Gambino) Mafia family.

Anastasia (1902–1957) was born in Italy and immigrated to New York in 1919. One year later, Prohibition offered bootleggers an unexpected cash bonanza, and Anastasia was one of those who got rich smuggling illegal whiskey. With his brother, Tony, he also muscled into the International Longshoreman's Union and seized virtual control of New York City's waterfront. When a new national crime syndicate organized during 1929–33, Anastasia became one of the mob's top enforcers, serving as second-in-command (under Louis "Lepke" Buchalter) of the deadly unit nicknamed "Murder, Incorporated."

Lepke died in the electric chair in 1944, leaving Anastasia in charge of the Brooklyn murder squad. Seven years later, after boss Vincent Mangano mysteriously vanished and his brother was murdered, Anastasia took control of the crime family. Soon, he became more erratic and violent than ever, causing some gangsters to call him "the Mad Hatter."

Anastasia did not know Willie Sutton, but after glimpsing Arnold Schuster on TV, he flew into a rage, shouting, "I hate squealers! Hit that guy!"[1] Three weeks later, on March 8, 1952, an unknown gunman ambushed Schuster outside his home, shooting him four times.

(continues)

(continued)

Ten years later, Mafia informer Joe Valachi revealed the facts of Schuster's death and named the triggerman as Frederick Tenuto, another FBI Top Ten fugitive whom Anastasia killed soon afterward, thereby ensuring that he could not squeal.

By the time Valachi spoke up, Anastasia had also been murdered. Other mob bosses, jealous of his power and frightened by his insane temper, ordered his death. On October 25, 1957, two gunmen executed Anastasia in a New York barbershop.

Diagram of the Brooklyn street where Arnold Schuster was slain. Mob boss Albert Anastasia ordered the hit after seeing on television that Schuster had snitched on bank robber Willie Sutton. *Bettmann/Corbis*

the gang's leader. Eleven days later, FBI agents added his name to the Bureau's new "Ten Most Wanted" fugitives list.

Normal procedure for Top Ten fugitives involved circulation of their photographs to newspapers and TV stations, plus display of

WANTED posters in local police stations and post offices. Remembering Sutton's taste for fine clothes, G-men also furnished his mug shots to various tailors.

Almost two years later, that tactic paid off.

CAPTURED

Arnold Schuster (1928–1952) was a tailor's son living in Brooklyn, New York. On February 18, 1952, he spotted Sutton on a subway train and followed him on foot to a service station, where Sutton bought a car battery. Schuster then informed police of Sutton's presence in the area. Soon officers swarmed the neighborhood, surprising Sutton as he installed the new battery in his car, parked on the street.

Although armed with two pistols, Sutton did not resist arrest. He denied committing any crimes since his escape in 1947, but detectives did not believe him. Two days later, they arrested Sutton's partners in the Queens raid, Thomas Kling (b. 1906) and John De Venuta.

De Venuta saved himself from prosecution by turning state's evidence against his friends. Jurors convicted Sutton and Kling of the Queens holdup on April 1, 1952. Both received 30-year terms for that crime, while Sutton got two additional 15-year terms on separate firearms charges. Since he already owed life plus 105 years to various state prisons, it seemed likely that Sutton would die behind bars.

A series of federal court rulings changed that, however, allowing Sutton's release on Christmas Eve 1969. His health was failing, and he had to live on welfare payments for a time, but Sutton still spoke out for prison reform. He earned a new living consulting with bankers about their security systems. In 1970 he made a TV commercial promoting a New England bank's new photo-I.D. credit cards.

In 1976 Sutton published a memoir, *Where the Money Was*. Although still denying his famous quotation, it served as an adequate title. Four years later, Willie the Actor died in Florida at age 79.

Most Wanted

Media fascination with "public enemies" faded quickly after the arrest of Alvin Karpis in 1936. A few more killings brought the era of celebrity bank robbers to an end. More fugitives were still at large, but 13 years elapsed before the FBI launched another media campaign to capture the worst.

William Hutchinson, editor in chief of the International News Service, was playing cards with J. Edgar Hoover in autumn 1949 when he suggested a story listing the "toughest guys" wanted by FBI agents. That story got so much publicity that Hoover decided to make it a permanent feature.

The FBI's first "Ten Most Wanted" list was published on March 14, 1950. Those listed included two murderers, six escaped convicts, and two men wanted for armed robbery. Willie Sutton (see Chapter 6), listed on March 20, was the 11th Top Ten fugitive, added after media reports produced the program's first arrest.

According to the FBI, Top Ten fugitives are those who, one, have a long record of serious crimes or are considered especially dangerous to society, and, two, whose capture may be aided by media coverage. Thus, bank robber Patty Hearst (Chapter 8) was *not* listed in 1974 because her case had already received worldwide publicity.

Since Hoover's death in 1972, Top Ten fugitives are chosen by FBI administrators from a list of candidates submitted by the bureau's 56 field offices. Those selected have no priority ranking—there is no "Number 1" except the first man ever listed (see below)—but still, some fugitives are *more wanted* than others. At press time for this book, the FBI offered a $6 million reward for terrorist Osama bin Laden (1957–), but only $1 million for Boston gangster James "Whitey" Bulger (1929–). Some rate no reward at all.

Once named, Top Ten fugitives remain on the list until they are captured, the charges against them are dropped (15 cases in 56 years), or the FBI decides that they no longer pose a danger to society. (Five have been cut because they are believed to be dead.) Fugitive murderer Donald Webb (1931–) has been listed since January 1981, but most members of the dishonor roll do not remain at large that long.

NUMBER ONE WITH A BULLET

Thomas James Holden (1895–1953), the FBI's first Top Ten fugitive in 1950, started robbing banks with partner Francis Keating in the 1920s. Members of the Holden-Keating gang included Harvey Bailey, Frank Nash, and Verne Miller (Chapters 3 and 4). A Chicago holdup sent Holden and Keating to Leavenworth prison in 1928, but they escaped three years later, with help from fellow inmate Machine Gun Kelly. Next, they joined the Barker-Karpis gang, but both were caught again in 1932 while golfing with Harvey Bailey in Kansas City. One of the arresting G-men, Agent Raymond Caffrey, died with Frank Nash 12 months later in the Kansas City massacre.

Finally paroled in November 1947, Holden returned to his native Chicago. Nineteen months later, during a drunken argument, he shot his wife and her two brothers. Facing triple murder charges, Holden fled, as he had always done before.

Despite publicity surrounding the FBI's first Top Ten list, it took G-men 15 months to find Holden. In June 1951, a resident of Beaverton, Oregon, recognized construction worker John McCullough as Holden. Convicted of murder in Chicago, Holden died in prison two years later.

THE BRINKS JOB

Two months before the Ten Most Wanted list was created, in January 1950, 11 men wearing Halloween masks invaded Boston's Brinks Building, stealing $2.8 million in cash and checks from the company's vault. Reporters called it the "crime of the century." The bandits vanished without a trace. The only clues left behind were a

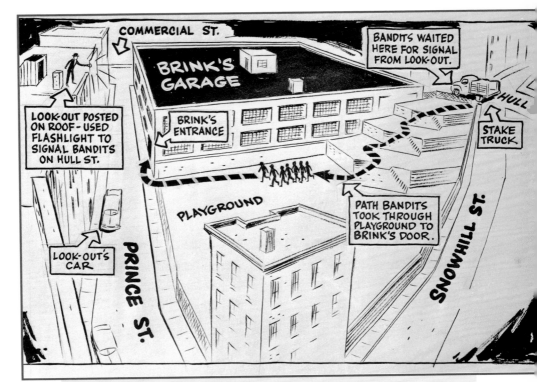

An artist's diagram depicting how the Brinks robbery was staged and executed. *Bettmann/Corbis*

cap, dropped by one of the thieves, and rope used to bind the Brinks guards.

While the Brinks holdup lasted a mere 15 minutes, it resulted from 12 months of planning. Several times, gang members crept into the Brinks Building at night, evading guards to chart the building's floor plan and defenses. Others robbed a burglar-alarm company, stealing samples of the same model used by Brinks in Boston. Finally, after six false starts, the thieves got it right.

Their plan was to sit on the loot for six years, until the statute of limitations expired, but gang member Joseph O'Keefe soon started grumbling that his share of the take was too small. In June 1950, O'Keefe and accomplice Stanley Gusciora were jailed for a Pennsylvania burglary. O'Keefe got three years on that charge, while Gusciora got five to 20. Both men demanded Brinks loot from the gang to finance their appeals.

In May 1952 ex-convict Alfred Gagnon named Carlton O'Brien as one of the Brinks job's planners. Three days later, unknown gunmen killed O'Brien. Meanwhile, Joe O'Keefe was free again, but facing more burglary charges. In December 1952 he named five Brinks suspects before a special grand jury. The five refused to testify and were jailed for contempt.

O'Keefe's former friends were fed up. They hired a hitman, Elmer "Trigger" Burke, to silence O'Keefe for good. Burke sprayed O'Keefe with machine-gun fire in June 1954, but O'Keefe survived his wounds and told all to the FBI. In January 1956 the grand jury

♀ STILL AT LARGE

Victor Manuel Gerena was born in 1958 and had a spotless record until age 25, but today we know that he led a double life, spending his free time with a group of Puerto Rican revolutionaries called *Los Macheteros* (the machete-wielders). That group claimed credit for killing two U.S. Navy officers in 1979, and for bombing jets at an Air Force base near San Juan in 1981.

On September 12, 1983, while working as a guard for Wells Fargo in West Hartford, Connecticut, Gerena pulled a gun on two fellow employees, handcuffed them, and injected them with drugs to make them sleep. He then opened the vault for intruders, fleeing with $7.1 million. *Los Macheteros* later claimed responsibility for the robbery.

FBI spokesmen added Gerena to the Top Ten list on May 14, 1984. In August 1985, G-men arrested 11 suspects in Puerto Rico, one in Mexico, and two in the United States. Alleged ringleader Filiberto Ojeda Rios (1933–2005) jumped bail and disappeared in 1990. He was later convicted in absentia and received a 55-year sentence. Four of the other 13 defendants were also convicted and sentenced to prison.

But the FBI still has not located Victor Gerena. He remains a Top Ten fugitive today, after 13 years on the list. Wells Fargo has offered a $250,000 reward for return of the stolen money, and $100,000 for information leading to Gerena's arrest.

filed 148 felony charges against nine surviving members of the Brinks gang. FBI agents bagged seven of the nine on January 12, 1956, but two remained at large.

Fugitive James Faherty (1912–) made the Top Ten list on March 19, 1956, while Thomas Richardson (1908–) followed on April 12. Despite the local heat, they stayed in Boston, sharing an apartment. G-men caught them together on May 16, 1956, seizing three guns and $5,000 in cash.

Stan Gusciora died before trial on the Brinks job convened. O'Keefe received a four-year sentence for cooperating with the prosecution, while his eight former friends were sentenced to life in prison. Most of the Brinks loot has never been found. Rumors persist that it is hidden somewhere in the hills outside Grand Rapids, Minnesota.

ALL-AMERICAN KILLER

Duane Pope (1943–) was every parent's dream: a soft-spoken boy who was respectful of his elders and attended church each Sunday. Pope also made good grades, while still finding time for athletics. In his senior year of college, he was captain of the football team. Pope graduated on May 30, 1965, at age 22.

Five days later, he went berserk.

At 11:15 a.m. on June 4, Pope entered the Farmers State Bank in Big Springs, Nebraska. He wore a business suit and carried a briefcase. Pope met bank president Andreas Kjelgaard and talked about a farm loan, then pulled a pistol from his briefcase and demanded cash.

Kjelgaard surrendered $1,598 from the cashier's station, but the bank's vault had a time lock and Pope could not afford to wait. He forced Kjelgaard and three bank employees to lie on the floor, side by side. Pope then shot each victim twice before leaving the bank. Andreas Kjelgaard and two others died. The lone survivor, Frank Kjelgaard (Andreas's relative), was paralyzed for life.

Pope's plan to leave no witnesses had failed. He had also made another clumsy mistake, renting the getaway car in his real name. Survivor Frank Kjelgaard identified photos of Pope, and G-men added his name to the Most Wanted list on June 11, 1965.

That same day, Pope surrendered to police in Kansas City. Jurors convicted him on three murder counts in March 1966, and he received a death sentence. Six years later, the United States Supreme Court overturned all existing death sentences in America, thereby reducing Pope's penalty to life imprisonment. He remains in custody today.

BRINGING THE WAR HOME

America's war in Vietnam (1965–1972) spawned many protests, some of them violent. While most anti-war activists were peaceful, some extremists tried to change U.S. policy by "bringing home the war" with acts of sabotage and terror. To support those efforts, some of them robbed banks.

College students Susan Saxe (1950–   ) and Katherine Ann Power (1949–   ) hated the war and tried to do something about it. First, in summer 1970, they stole a carload of automatic weapons from a military arsenal in Massachusetts. Next, they took $6,240 at gunpoint from a bank in Philadelphia.

Disappointed by that score, the two young women recruited three career criminals—Stanley Bond (1945–1972), William Gilday (1929–   ), and Robert Valeri (1949–   )—to help with their next holdup. Power stayed with the backup getaway car on September 21, while Saxe and their three gunmen struck a bank in Boston. This time, they bagged $26,000—but they also killed a policeman.

The heat was fierce. Bond, Gilday, and Valeri were all soon arrested and named their female accomplices. The FBI had never heard of Saxe or Power. Neither one had a criminal record, but both made the Most Wanted list—expanded during the "radical" era to include 16 fugitives—on October 17, 1970.

Gilday received a life sentence for murder. Bond and Valeri received shorter terms for manslaughter and robbery. Bond later died when a homemade bomb exploded in his prison cell.

Meanwhile, G-men kept looking for Saxe and Power. Philadelphia police found Susan Saxe in March 1975. Three months later, jurors convicted her of robbery and manslaughter. She was paroled in 1982 and disappeared.

The FBI removed Power from its Top Ten list in June 1984. A Boston prosecutor explained: "Of the five, the weakest case is against her, and it's been so long, who'd want to prosecute her now?"[1]

That question was answered in September 1993, when Power surrendered to Boston police after 23 years in hiding. She had moved

Susan Edith Saxe in a 1970 FBI Most Wanted poster. *AP Photo/FBI*

to Oregon, changed her name, married, and had a 16-year-old son. Power pled guilty to various charges and received a sentence of eight to 12 years in prison, plus 20 years probation. The court also banned her from selling her story for profit.

WHO'S NEXT?

The FBI's Most Wanted list presents an ever-changing cast of characters. From traditional bandits, kidnappers, and killers in the 1950s, it grew to include political activists in the 1960s and 1970s, serial killers and members of organized crime in the 1980s, and terrorists and child-molesters in the 1990s and 2000s. The Bureau's priorities change with events and political trends.

As of December 7, 2007, 489 fugitives have found places on the Ten Most Wanted list. Of those, 456 have been found, either dead or alive. Tips from citizens responding to publicity resulted in

147 captures. Several of those were located through joint efforts of the FBI and TV program *America's Most Wanted*. In our information culture, there is truly nowhere to hide. To view the Ten Most Wanted list, see this Web site: http://www.fbi.gov/wanted/topten/fugitives/fugitives.htm.

White Terror

Susan Saxe and Katherine Power were neither the first nor the last bandits to rob banks in the name of some political cause. Others who have followed the same path include Marxists and fascists, black militants and white supremacists. In the early 1980s, a tiny neo-Nazi group robbed banks and armored cars to fund a war against the U.S. government in Washington, D.C.

THE WARRIOR

Robert Jay Mathews (1953–1984) was an angry young man who blamed the failures of his life on Jews and Communists. He joined the radical John Birch Society at age 11 and then dropped out of high school to lead a small militia group, the Sons of Liberty. That group fell apart when members started arguing about religion. In 1973 Mathews was sentenced to six months probation for evading income taxes.

In 1974 Mathews moved to rural Washington State and became a polygamist (one who has multiple wives). Soon, he forged ties to the Aryan Nations, in nearby Idaho, and to William Pierce's racist National Alliance. In 1978 Pierce published a novel, *The Turner Diaries*, which describes an America controlled by ZOG—the Zionist Occupation Government, secretly run by Israel. In the novel, a group of resistance fighters called The Order bomb government buildings and execute "race traitors" to defend the white master race.

Some authorities believe that *The Turner Diaries* inspired terrorist Timothy McVeigh (1968–2001) to bomb Oklahoma City's federal building in April 1995, killing 168 persons. However,

Robert Mathews was the first to use the novel as a blueprint for a life of crime.

THE ORDER

While visiting the Aryan Nations compound during 1982–1983, Mathews recruited other racists like himself to join a new resistance

⚲ NOT-SO-FUNNY MONEY

The Order was not the first group to use counterfeit money against its enemies. In fact, various governments have used fake currency to destabilize hostile nations for more than 200 years.

During the American Revolution (1775–1783), Great Britain printed so many fake Continental dollars that some merchants in the rebellious colonies refused to accept government currency. British general William Howe maintained a special counterfeiting unit and bundles of bogus Continental currency were advertised for sale in Tory newspapers loyal to the British crown. On one occasion in April 1770, Continental troops in New Jersey captured eight British soldiers with 45,000 counterfeit Continental dollars.

During the American Civil War (1861–65), Union counterfeiters turned out large quantities of fake Confederate bills which, ironically, were often of a higher quality than legitimate notes printed below the Mason-Dixon Line. Vermont native Samuel Upham (1819–1885) was the premier Union counterfeiter, starting with a batch of 3,000 $5 bills, which he sold for a penny apiece in February 1862. By year's end Upham had a full range of phony Confederate notes in circulation, along with bogus postage stamps. Northern officials suspected him of counterfeiting Union currency as well, but Upham denied it and U.S. Secretary of War Edwin Stanton intervened to dismiss the case. Upham's counterfeit notes infuriated Confederate leaders, who imposed the death penalty for counterfeiting, but they were unable to suppress the traffic in counterfeit bills.

In the 1920s Hungarian officials sought to avenge their nation's territorial losses to France during World War I (1914–18) by printing and circulating 10 million counterfeit 1,000-franc notes. Agents from two other losing nations, Austria and Germany, movement against ZOG. His followers included members of the Aryan Nations, Ku Klux Klan, National Alliance, and an Arkansas-based group called the Covenant, Sword, and Arm of the Lord (CSA). Altogether, 27 men and three women joined The Order, also known to members as the Silent Brotherhood.

The Order started small, robbing a Seattle video store of $369. Next, the rebels turned to counterfeiting, but the $50 bills they

joined in the conspiracy, according to reports filed by the League of Nations, and six members of the counterfeiting ring were jailed in Holland during 1926. The fake bills rarely passed inspection, since France printed its currency on exotic raw paper material imported from one of its foreign colonies.

During World War II (1939–45) Nazi Germany launched "Operation Bernhard"—named for its originator, Maj. Bernhard Krüger (1904–89)—using 142 Jewish artists at the Sachsenhausen concentration camp to design counterfeit British currency. Starting in 1942, the Germans printed British pound notes valued at £134,610,810 ($377 million) and shipped them out to 100 Nazi agents worldwide. According to one member of the captive team, convicted counterfeiter Adolf Burger, Operation Bernhard also produced 200 fake American $100 bills in February 1945, but Sachsenhausen was evacuated before large quantities were printed. The Nazis moved their counterfeiting plant to Mauthausen, but U.S. troops liberated that camp in May 1945 and thus foiled the plan.

Today, U.S. Treasury spokesmen say that North Korea produces the highest-quality counterfeit American currency (dubbed "Superdollars"), while private operators in Bulgaria and Colombia also produce significant amounts of fake U.S. money. In 2006 India's Central Bureau of Intelligence charged that a Pakistani government printing press in Quetta had produced large quantities of counterfeit Indian currency, smuggled into India as part of long-running hostilities between the two nations. Indian authorities also claimed that Pakistan furnished counterfeit Indian notes free of charge to criminals in Dubai, and that counterfeit money was used to finance terrorist bombings in Mumbai, India, that killed 209 persons and wounded more than 700 on July 11, 2006.

printed were of such poor quality that member Bruce Pierce was arrested the first time he tried to spend one. Finally, Mathews decided that the group's best hope for income was bank robbery.

He pulled the first holdup alone, stealing $25,952 from a Seattle bank in December 1983, but an exploding dye pack ruined most of the loot. Next, in January 1984, Order members stole $3,600 from a bank in Spokane, Washington. They sent $100 to Aryan Nations chief Richard Butler, and $200 to Michigan Klan leader Robert Miles.

The bandits improved with practice. In March 1984 they robbed an armored truck in Seattle, escaping with $43,345. A month later, they scored $230,379 from another armored truck in Northgate, a Seattle suburb. (Mathews sent another $40,000 to the Aryan Nations.) In July 1984 an 11-man team stopped a Brinks truck near Ukiah, California, and stole $3.6 million.

Despite complaints from some of his followers, Mathews donated nearly half the Brinks loot to racist leaders including Butler, Miles, Pierce, Glenn Miller (of the White Patriot Party), Tom Metzger (White Aryan Resistance), and Louis Beam (Aryan Nations "ambassador at large").

While robbery was profitable, The Order still saw its main function as fighting the "Jewish conspiracy." In June 1984 three members murdered Alan Berg, a Jewish talk-show host in Denver who often insulted Nazis and Klansmen on his radio program. Mathews saw the murder as a victory, but his little army was already running out of time.

DOWNFALL

Despite their success at armed robbery, members of The Order also kept printing poor-quality counterfeit cash. In June 1984 FBI agents jailed member Tom Martinez for passing fake money and Martinez agreed to betray his friends in return for dismissal of all charges.

Martinez arranged a meeting with Mathews in Portland, Oregon, on November 24. FBI agents were waiting when Mathews arrived with sidekick Gary Yarbrough (1955–   ). A shootout ensued, and Mathews escaped, but agents captured Yarbrough.

Soon afterward, Mathews and his remaining followers issued a declaration of war against ZOG. Instead of attacking, however, they scattered across the country. Mathews fled with three others to Whidbey Island, in Washington's Puget Sound. FBI agents followed him there and arrested his companions, but Mathews chose to fight. He died on December 8, 1984, in a furious battle with G-men.

More arrests followed. By the end of 1985, 15 members of The Order pled guilty on various charges, while jurors convicted 13 more in state and federal trials. Six of those who pled guilty received suspended sentences. The rest drew prison terms ranging from three to 250 years. CSA leader James Ellison and five of his followers also pled guilty to supplying The Order with illegal weapons.

The sweep was a government victory, but prosecutors still wanted to punish the racists who profited from The Order's crime spree.

SEDITION

In April 1987 a federal grand jury indicted 17 defendants for sedition (conspiracy to overthrow a government). Those charged included five members of The Order, six members of the CSA, a gun dealer who allegedly supplied arms to the bandits, and various racists who accepted money from Mathews—Beam, Butler, Ellison, Miles, and Miller.

Louis Beam fled the country and was placed on the FBI's Most Wanted list. G-men and Mexican police caught him at Guadalajara, after a shootout in November 1987. Meanwhile, Ellison and Miller both agreed to testify against their former allies.

The trial began at Fort Smith, Arkansas, in April 1988. Aside from Ellison and Miller, prosecution witnesses included Tom Martinez and three other ex-Order members. The judge quickly dismissed charges filed against the gun dealer, and jurors acquitted the other 13 defendants of all counts on April 7.

Prosecutors were stunned, while some of those accused went home to celebrate. For 10 of them, however, there would be no party. They went back to prison to complete their sentences for other crimes. One, Richard Snell, was executed in April 1995 for the murder of an Arkansas policeman.

THE NIGHTMARE CONTINUES

Neo-Nazi terrorism did not end with The Order's collapse in 1985. Even before most members had faced trial for their crimes, a new group—dubbed The Order II—was organized in Idaho. Members set off several bombs and planned to murder witness Tom Martinez, but they soon joined their idols in prison.

A more efficient group is the Phineas Priesthood, named for a biblical character who killed a mixed-race couple in Numbers 25:6–11. Phineas spokesman Richard Kelly Hoskins (1928–   ) outlined the group's violent program in his book *Vigilantes of Christendom* (1990). Members have been linked to various crimes, including bank robbery, bombings, and conspiracy to kill FBI agents.

In August 1991 police jailed self-described Phineas priest Walter Thody (1939–   ) for stealing $52,000 from a thrift shop in Muskogee, Oklahoma. Thody, who received a life sentence in 1992, claimed the robbery was meant to finance executions of various "Jewish conspirators."

Five years later, in October 1996, authorities in Spokane, Washington, charged four Phineas priests with robbing two banks and bombing various targets, including the local Planned Parenthood office. Three defendants received life sentences, while the fourth got 55 years.

More efficient still was the Aryan Republican Army (ARA), whose members robbed 22 banks across the American Midwest during 1994–1995. Leader Peter Langan (1958–   ), alias "Commander Pedro," issued videotapes of himself holding a copy of *Vigilantes of Christendom*, declaring the work his handbook of revolution. ARA members also studied *The Turner Diaries* and subscribed to the tenets of "Christian Identity," a racist cult that believes Jews are the physical children of Satan.

As with The Order, the ARA was betrayed by one of its own. Member Richard Lee Guthrie (1958–1996), an ex-Navy SEAL, was under surveillance for threatening President George H. W. Bush in 1991. FBI agents soon linked him to the ARA's series of bank robberies. He agreed to help the government, as a result of which Langan was wounded and captured in January 1996, after a shootout with G-men in Ohio. Two other ARA members, Kevin McCarthy and Scott Stedeford, were also arrested.

Guthrie pled guilty to 19 holdups and agreed to testify against his friends. He then hanged himself in his jail cell. McCarthy and Stedeford *did* testify against Langan, resulting in a prison term of life plus 55 years for Commander Pedro. Mark Thomas, an aging neo-Nazi leader from Pennsylvania, also pled guilty to helping the

ARA plan its raids. He received an eight-year sentence and was freed in early 2004.

Meanwhile, in May 2001, an FBI report described Oklahoma City bomber Timothy McVeigh as an ARA member, claiming that he participated in several holdups to finance his own terrorist plans. McVeigh's sister confirms that he once gave her cash that he claimed was bank loot. So far, no ARA members have been charged with participating in the Oklahoma bombing.

CRIMINAL OR VICTIM?

Another group of political bandits, active during 1973–1975, was the Symbionese Liberation Army (SLA). Although the group only had 13 members at peak strength, it captured global attention and terrorized the state of California before its leaders literally went up in smoke.

The SLA began in prison as the Black Cultural Association, designed to politically educate African-American inmates. Oddly, most of the counselors were white. One of them, William Wolfe, befriended inmate Donald DeFreeze and may have helped him escape in March 1973.

DeFreeze (1943–1974), calling himself "Field Marshal Cinque," soon formed the SLA. Its name derives from *symbiosis* (cooperation among living things), and its symbol was a seven-headed cobra. By autumn 1973 DeFreeze had recruited 10 more warriors for his "army," including seven young women. All were white, but some wore Afro wigs and dark makeup to disguise their race. They adopted revolutionary code names and armed themselves for war.

In November 1973 the SLA killed Oakland's black superintendent of schools, Marcus Foster. Police arrested the shooters two months later, prompting DeFreeze to plan a prisoner exchange. On February 4 the gang kidnapped newspaper heiress Patricia Hearst (1954–   ) from her Berkeley apartment.

Authorities refused to trade their prisoners for Hearst, so DeFreeze asked for ransom instead. Hearst's family agreed to distribute free food in various California ghettos, but the program ended after a riot broke out in one neighborhood.

On April 15, 1974, SLA members robbed San Francisco's Hibernia Bank, wounding two bystanders and escaping with $10,960. Witnesses and surveillance videos identified Patty Hearst as one of

OFFICE OF THE DIRECTOR

UNITED STATES DEPARTMENT OF JUSTICE

FEDERAL BUREAU OF INVESTIGATION

WASHINGTON, D.C. 20535

April 19, 1974

RE: **DONALD DAVID DE FREEZE**　　**PATRICIA MICHELLE SOLTYSIK**　　　　　　　**PATRICIA CAMPBELL HEARST**
　　　NANCY LING PERRY　　　　　**CAMILLA CHRISTINE HALL**　　　　　　　　　　**MATERIAL WITNESS**

TO WHOM IT MAY CONCERN:

The FBI is conducting an investigation to determine the whereabouts of these individuals whose descriptions and photographs appear below. Federal warrants charging robbery of a San Francisco bank on April 15, 1974, have been issued at San Francisco, California, for Camilla Hall, Donald DeFreeze, Nancy Perry, and Patricia Soltysik. A material witness warrant in this robbery has been issued for Patricia Hearst, who was abducted from her Berkeley, California, residence on February 4, 1974, by a group which has identified itself as the Symbionese Liberation Army (SLA). The participants in the bank robbery also claim to be members of the SLA.

DONALD DAVID DE FREEZE
N/M, DOB 11/16/43, 5'9" to 5'11",
150-160, blk hair, br eyes

PATRICIA MICHELLE SOLTYSIK
W/F, DOB 5/17/50, 5'3" to 5'4",
116, dk br hair, br eyes

PATRICIA CAMPBELL HEARST
W/F, DOB 2/20/54, 5'3", 110,
lt br hair, br eyes

MATERIAL WITNESS

NANCY LING PERRY
W/F, DOB 9/19/47, 5', 95-105, red
br hair, haz eyes

CAMILLA CHRISTINE HALL
W/F, DOB 3/24/45, 5'6", 125,
blonde hair, blue eyes

If you have any information concerning these individuals, please notify your local FBI office, a telephone listing for which can be found on the first page of your directory. In view of the crimes for which these individuals are being sought, they should be considered armed and extremely dangerous, and no action should be taken which would endanger anyone's safety.

Very truly yours,

C m Kelley

Clarence M. Kelley

FBI flyer on Symbionese Liberation Army members Donald Defreeze, Patricia Soltysik, Nancy Perry, and Camilla Hall, and kidnapped newspaper heiress Patricia Hearst released in April 1974. *AP Photo*

the raiders, holding a rifle and cursing bank customers. Audiotapes from Hearst—who now called herself Tania—confirmed her support for the SLA.

On May 17 police traced the gang to a house in Los Angeles. A fierce battle ensued, ending only when the house burned down.

Inside, DeFreeze and five companions died—but Patty Hearst was not among them.

She resurfaced nearly a year later on April 21, 1975, driving a getaway car when four other SLA members robbed a bank in Carmichael, California, stealing $15,000 and killing innocent bystander Myrna Opsahl in the process. On September 18, 1975, G-men finally caught Hearst in San Francisco, with three other SLA members.

At trial in early 1976, Hearst claimed that she was drugged, raped, and "brainwashed" by her kidnappers, forced to join the SLA against her will. However, on the witness stand, she claimed her Fifth Amendment privilege against self-incrimination 19 times when asked about other holdups.

Jurors convicted Hearst and she received a seven-year sentence. She served two years before President Jimmy Carter released her from prison. President Bill Clinton officially pardoned Hearst in 2001.

Other SLA members were less fortunate. William (1949–) and Emily (1947–) Harris were convicted of auto theft, kidnapping, and robbery, serving seven years. Russell Little (1949–) and Joseph Remiro received life terms for murdering Marcus Foster in Oakland. Kathleen Soliah dodged police until 1999, then received a sentence of 10 years to life for conspiracy. In February 2003 Soliah, the Harrises, Michael Bortin (1949–), and James Kilgore (1948–) were sentenced for the 1975 bank holdup and murder. Their prison terms ranged from six to 14 years. In 2004 Kilgore received another 54 months on fraud and explosives charges.

Armed
and Dangerous

Throughout history, criminals have pioneered the use of new technology and weapons, while law enforcement lags behind. "Motorized" bandits drove getaway cars when most police forces still used horse-drawn wagons. Gangsters used machine guns and other military weapons while police were armed with six-shooters. The FBI's Computer Crimes Unit was formed *six years* after the Internet brought about the age of global cybercrime.

Criminals lead the way in technological advances for several reasons. First, unlike police, their budgets are not fixed by politicians who pinch pennies and debate a problem endlessly before attempting to solve it. Second, criminals are generally less conservative than law enforcement officers. They welcome change and seek new ways to profit from it, while police and lawmakers more often drag their feet, clinging to visions of the "good old days." And third, police work, *by its very nature,* is reactive in most cases. Officers cannot investigate a crime before it happens, and lawmakers only ban particular items or activities when problems are reported. Sometimes, in police work, progress follows tragedy.

MIAMI MADNESS

William Russell Matix (1951–1986) and Michael Lee Platt (1954–1986) met in 1974 while serving in the U.S. Army. Matix was an officer in the Military Police and had spent four years in the Marine Corps before switching to the Army. Platt had been a star athlete in high school and enlisted after graduation.

The two men became friends and more. Years later, FBI agents suggested that they were also wife-killers, plotting together to murder Platt's wife in December 1983 and Matix's in December 1984. Both men collected life insurance and settled in Miami, Florida, where they began new lives of crime.

During their first holdup, in May 1985, they bagged $100,000 from a Wells Fargo armored truck. In June of that year, they looted another Wells Fargo truck, stealing $40,000 and killing the driver. Four months later, they murdered a Miami man and stole his Chevrolet Monte Carlo, using it in five more robberies between October 1985 and March 1986.

Two of those holdups went badly. On October 16 they wounded an armored truck's driver and then fled empty-handed. One day later another truck's driver fired on the bandits, forcing them to run.

Platt and Matix did better on November 8, stealing $41,469 from a local bank. Two months later, they raided a Brinks truck outside another bank, wounding the driver and bagging $54,000. In March 1986 they returned to the same crime scene, this time looting the bank itself of $8,338.

By now, FBI agents knew the bandits were driving a murder victim's Monte Carlo, armed with an automatic rifle, a shotgun, and several pistols. Miami agents mobilized their C-1 "reactive" unit, a team created to prowl the streets and respond at top speed to reports of crimes in progress.

On April 11, the C-1 unit's 14 agents were assigned to watch four different banks in the district where Matix and Platt had committed their crimes. At 9:20 a.m., Agents Jerry Dove and Ben Grogan spotted the Monte Carlo. They trailed it for several blocks, reporting to the other members of their squad by radio, before they turned on their flashers and siren.

A high-speed chase began, with Platt and Matix weaving through traffic while six more G-men in four cars joined the pursuit. After several miles, the bandits swerved onto a side street, only to discover that it was a dead-end cul-de-sac. Platt and Matix were trapped, but they were not ready to surrender.

FIREFIGHT

The next few minutes of the fight are often described as the bloodiest in FBI history. Michael Platt opened fire with an automatic rifle, quickly wounding Agents Gordon McNeil and Edmundo Mireles. Agents Grogan and McNeil returned fire with their pistols, striking William Matix in the head, neck, and wrist.

Platt left his car and was hit three times by shots from Agents Dove and Gil Orrantia, but the wounds did not stop him. He drew a pistol and shot McNeil again, leaving him paralyzed. Matix pinned down Agents Dove and Grogan with shotgun fire, while Platt rushed in to kill them, also wounding Agent John Hanlon.

Platt and Matix next piled into one of the FBI cars, intending to flee while the agents were dying or dazed. Agent Mireles, despite his disabled left arm, grabbed a shotgun and fired five blasts at the bandits, then advanced with his .38 caliber pistol and finished them off at close range.

When the smoke cleared, two FBI agents were dead and five more were wounded. Only Agent Ron Risner survived the firefight without injury. Autopsy reports show that Platt suffered 12 gunshot wounds, while Matix was hit six times, including five shots to the face and neck. Despite speculation that drugs helped the bandits fight on despite wounding, blood tests showed their systems were clean.

After the shootout, FBI spokesmen told reporters they were searching Miami for others involved in the Platt-Matix crime spree. Witnesses reported three masked bandits at the first holdup scene, in April 1985, but no accomplices were ever identified.

The FBI would learn from its worst-ever day (see sidebar), but other agencies were slow to absorb the grim lesson. Even the supermodern Los Angeles Police Department (LAPD), with its famous SWAT (Special Weapons And Tactics) team, was caught unprepared when a similar battle erupted 11 years later.

GUN CRAZY

Los Angeles recorded 1,126 bank robberies in 1996, including 222 "take-overs" where armed bandits seized control in the style of Jesse James and John Dillinger. Even so, deaths and woundings were rare, and most bank robbers were quickly arrested. Most, but not all.

Two of L.A.'s more successful bandits were Emil Dechebal Matasareanu (1966–1997) and Larry Eugene Phillips Jr. (1970–1997). Matasareanu was born in Romania and came to America with his parents. He grew up in a small mental hospital run by his mother, and suffered brain damage when one of the patients struck him. As a result, he had epileptic seizures until surgery corrected his condition in July 1996.

Larry Phillips was a real estate agent, married with two children. He met Matasareanu at a local gym. Both men were bodybuilders, and they also shared an obsession with guns. Their strange friendship soon blossomed into crime.

In October 1993 police stopped the pair for speeding and got a surprise. In Matasareanu's car, the officers found two automatic rifles, four pistols, 1,600 rounds of ammunition, six smoke grenades, disguises, a police radio scanner, and $244 in a plastic Sears bag. While no robbery was proved, both men pled guilty on weapons charges. Matasareanu served 71 days in jail, while Phillips served 99.

The arrests did not discourage Matasareanu and Phillips. They went on to rob an armored truck of $23,000 in Denver, and then looted another in L.A. for $125,000. Their third holdup failed when an armored truck's driver refused to stop at their roadblock, but they rebounded by stealing $750,000 from a Los Angeles bank. On their fifth outing, they mimicked Miami's Matix and Platt, returning to the scene of their second armored truck robbery but raiding the bank instead, escaping with another $790,000.

Many bandits would have been satisfied with those hauls, but Matasareanu and Phillips wanted more. Their next job, they decided, would be even bigger.

And they would have plenty of guns.

BLAZE OF GLORY

In preparation for their next heist, Phillips cut up several armored vests, stitching homemade bulletproof suits that would cover each bandit from neck to ankles. The final product weighed 42 pounds. In addition, Matasareanu and Phillips armed themselves with four

♀ UNARMED ROBBERY

Most bank robbers may not qualify as criminal masterminds, but they *do* keep track of legislation affecting their chosen careers. Today, federal statutes treat use of a weapon during bank robberies as an "aggravating circumstance" that demands longer prison terms with no allowance for probation or early release from prison on "good behavior."

Accordingly, it seems that a majority of modern bandits enter banks with nothing but a note, demanding cash and the potential threat of force, leaving their guns, bombs, or other weapons at home. Journalist Bradley Hope reports that 91.5 percent of New York's bank holdups in 2006 (a total of 260) were "note robberies," while only 24 cases involved display of weapons.[1]

While unarmed robbery may reduce a thief's prison sentence, note-passing alone does not ensure successful holdups. In fact, the note itself may help convict a robber if left behind with fingerprints or other forensic evidence or if later found in a suspect's possession. Sheriff's deputies in Nassau County, New York, arrested a female suspect in August 2007 on charges of stealing $1,600 from a local Bank of America branch. At the arrest, officers found loot from the bank and several drafts of the holdup note, prepared as the suspect was trying to find the right words for her task.

Michigan bank robber Brian Lockhart did not plan ahead for his December 2007 robbery of a bank in Mahtomedi, Minnesota. Instead, he scrawled a note on one of the bank's deposit slips and passed it to a teller, who surrendered an undisclosed amount of cash. Bank employees gave police Lockhart's description and officers found him nearby, pockets stuffed with money—and the handwritten note.

Note-passing robberies may also lead to additional, unexpected charges, as when Leland Snyder robbed a bank in Muskegon, Michigan, in March 2007. Surprised by police as he left the bank, Snyder shoved the note into his mouth and tried to swallow it, then bit the fingers of an officer who grappled to retrieve it. The bite produced additional felony charges of resisting arrest and causing injury to an officer while obstructing police.

automatic rifles and thousands of armor-piercing bullets. They were ready for war.

At 9:15 a.m. on February 28, 1997, Matasareanu and Phillips invaded a Bank of America branch in North Hollywood, shouting threats at 10 employees and 32 customers. They clubbed one man with a rifle butt and then bagged $303,305 from the vault. Disappointed by the relatively small take, Matasareanu tried to open the bank's automatic teller safe, but a time lock frustrated him. A burst of bullets from his rifle jammed the lock completely, sending him into a rage.

Outside, a passerby had seen the holdup in progress and flagged down a police car. Phillips watched and warned Matasareanu as more officers arrived. Soon, 370 SWAT and patrol officers surrounded the bank.

After locking their 32 hostages inside the vault, Matasareanu and Phillips split up. Phillips emerged from the bank's north door at 9:38 a.m., and Matasareanu left the south door seconds later, dragging a sack of money behind him. Suddenly, three dye packs exploded in the bag, spewing red smoke and ruining the money.

Both bandits raised their rifles and opened fire.

Police fought back with shotguns and pistols, but their hits barely fazed the armored gunmen. Wounded officers and bystanders began to drop along the street. Police dodged from one car to another, ducking armor-piercing bullets. Some retreated into nearby shops. Others raced to a nearby gun store, commandeering high-powered rifles to replace their standard-issue weapons.

Matasareanu suffered a leg wound as he reached his getaway car, but he climbed in and continued firing through its windows. Phillips reached the car moments later, opening the trunk and swapping his empty rifle for another. A police bullet struck his new semiautomatic weapon, but instead of disabling the gun, the shot converted it to more deadly full-automatic fire.

Phillips remained on foot, while Matasareanu kept pace with the getaway car. By that time, news helicopters were circling overhead, broadcasting the battle live to a worldwide television audience. Phillips fired at one of the helicopters, then stopped to reload.

A police bullet struck Phillips in the left shoulder, disabling one arm, but he still walked to the trunk of his getaway car and retrieved a third rifle, firing it one-handed. Matasareanu opened the passenger's door, but Phillips refused to get in. While Phillips

Los Angeles police and one civilian take cover as bank robbers Emil Dechebal Matasareanu and Larry Eugene Phillips Jr. are confronted at a Bank of America in the North Hollywood section of Los Angeles on February 28, 1997. *AP Photo/Los Angeles Daily News, Gene Blevins*

distracted police, Matasareanu drove past their barricade at the end of the block.

Finally, some 40 minutes into the firefight, Phillips's rifle jammed. He dropped it, drew a pistol, and fired four more shots at police before shooting himself in the head.

Matasareanu drove on until police bullets flattened his tires. He stopped a passing pickup truck at gunpoint, let its driver flee, then limped back to his bullet-riddled car for yet another rifle. Climbing into the pickup, he found that its owner had taken the keys when he fled. Just then, a SWAT van pulled up nearby. Matasareanu exchanged more shots with the police until a storm of bullets brought him down at last.

What happened next is unclear. Some witnesses (and members of Matasareanu's family) claim that angry officers beat the wounded robber and let him bleed to death before allowing ambulance attendants to reach him. Police say that Matasareanu died quickly from various wounds, without any abuse.

This much we know: Matasareanu and Phillips fired 1,110 shots in the battle. No final estimate of police rounds fired was

♀ LEARNING FROM TRAGEDY

Both the FBI and LAPD conducted studies of their respective firefights in 1986 and 1997. The FBI Academy's three-day Wound Ballistics Seminar at Quantico, Virginia, concluded that Matix and Platt did not die immediately from their initial wounds because ammunition used by G-men was not powerful enough.

Accordingly, the FBI abandoned its standard .38-caliber pistols, used by most agents since 1933, and issued .40-caliber semiautomatic handguns instead. Those weapons have greater stopping power and higher ammunition capacity, holding 10 shots instead of a normal revolver's six rounds.

Studies of the North Hollywood battle focused on a different problem, namely the best means of stopping gunmen dressed in body armor. LAPD concluded that standard 12-gauge shotgun rounds, together with .38-caliber or 9mm pistol ammunition, were inadequate to penetrate bullet-resistant fabrics such as Kevlar. As a result of that study, selected patrol officers in Los Angeles and elsewhere across the nation now carry in their vehicles military-style .223-caliber rifles, similar to the M-16 used by American troops in combat. Those weapons use 20- or 30-round magazines, fire up to 950 rounds per minute in full-auto mode, and generate a muzzle velocity of 3,250 feet per second.

ever produced. Matasareanu suffered 29 wounds, while Phillips was hit 11 times. Twelve officers and eight civilians were also shot, but all survived. In 1998 the LAPD awarded 17 Medals of Valor to various officers for their actions in the firefight.

Following the shootout, Matasareanu's family sued the LAPD for wrongful death for withholding medical treatment. The first trial ended with a jury deadlock, after which the family dropped its case. Anti-gun activists also sued the gun shop that loaned weapons to police officers during the firefight, noting that the shop owner ignored laws requiring a 10-day waiting period before delivery of weapons. The case was finally dismissed, but the cost of legal defense forced the shop out of business. In 2003 a film titled *44 Minutes: The North Hollywood Shoot-Out* was released, dramatizing the events of the bloody, failed bank robbery.

An ATF firearms examiner displays a .223 caliber rifle. After the North Hollywood gunfight with Matasareanu and Phillips, selected patrol officers across the United States carry this rifle in case of an encounter with criminals wearing full body armor. *AP Photo/Matt Houston*

Prevention
and Investigation

Thieves have schemed to rob banks for as long as banks have existed. Banks are responsible for preventing robberies, while law enforcement agencies investigate bank holdups after they occur. Bank personnel have no special authority to arrest thieves who escape from the crime scene, and police generally play no part in guarding banks before a robbery (although they may offer advice on security).

UNDER LOCK AND KEY

Before 1866 all recorded bank robberies were actually burglaries, committed during hours when the target banks were closed. Thieves broke in through doors or windows, chiseled through walls, or tunneled through floors at night, on weekends, or on holidays. The initial bankers' response was to construct banks using thicker, tougher building materials, including various kinds of stone, concrete, and metal. In time, however, would-be bandits overcame each innovation.

Locks are central to any bank. Aside from securing its outer doors against intruders, they also protect rooms, drawers, and cash deposits inside the bank. Keys control simple locks, but most of those can be opened by any locksmith—or broken, with sufficient brute force.

Combination locks were next employed, restricting knowledge of key numbers to selected banking personnel. Modern keypad locks are a variant of the combination system. Combination locks may be defeated with various mechanical or electronic devices that detect the critical numbers.

Time locks, pioneered in the nineteenth century, include clockwork devices that prevent a lock from opening before a preselected time. Their first—and still most common—application is in banking. Duane Pope (Chapter 7) was one of many American bandits who have been frustrated by time locks.

Early bankers soon discovered that locked doors alone would not protect their money. The next step was construction of a safe,

A group of people walk out through the main door of the Bank of Japan vault during a tour. *AP Photo/Katsumi Kasahara*

defined as any secure, lockable box used for storing cash or other valuables. Safes come in all sizes and are made from steel or other materials designed to resist thieves, fire, and other elements (water, dust, etc.) that may damage their contents.

Brothers Charles (1779–1846) and Jeremiah Chubb (1793–1860) began designing safes in 1818 and patented the first "burglar-proof" safe in 1835. Needless to say, safecrackers soon found ways to open safes illegally, including the use of various drills and explosives. In some cases, thieves equipped with winches and trucks stole whole safes. In a modern variation on this technique, thieves have been known to steal entire automated teller machines for the cash stored inside.

The largest safes are known as vaults or strong rooms. A vault is the central feature of most modern banks, secured by massive steel doors. Walls, ceilings, and floors include steel-reinforced concrete, sometimes with additional steel plates. The largest known vault door in use today is found at the Fourth District Federal Reserve bank in Cleveland, Ohio. It is 18 feet 10 inches tall and weighs 47 tons.

Such vaults offer the closest thing to true security. In August 1945, four Mosler Safe Company vaults at a bank in Hiroshima, Japan, survived with their contents undamaged 100 yards from the detonation point of the first atomic bomb. Most bank vaults now include sophisticated time locks, plus vents to provide air for anyone who is accidentally locked inside.

Within bank vaults, further security is provided by safe deposit boxes, where individual customers store personal items that may not be safe in their homes. Thieves who manage to penetrate bank vaults sometimes open the safe deposit boxes, seeking private stashes of money, jewels, or other valuables.

INTERNAL SECURITY

Stout walls and locks are not enough to outwit determined thieves. Since the nineteenth century, most banks also have been equipped with various kinds of alarms to summon help during a robbery.

The earliest burglar alarms were set to make noise after hours if intruders broke into the bank. Their clamor would alert police officers on patrol, and hopefully scare away thieves. As daylight robberies became more common, hidden triggers were installed to let bank employees sound alarms with a robbery in progress. When

♀ AMERICA'S MOST WANTED

John Walsh became a reluctant crime fighter in 1981 when his six-year-old son was murdered in Florida. That brutal crime remains officially unsolved. While assisting police with his own case, Walsh gained awareness of other missing children and fugitives at large, sparing no effort to crack unsolved cases and bring fleeing felons to justice.

The final result, premiering on the Fox network in February 1988, was *America's Most Wanted,* a weekly program that profiles dangerous fugitives and missing persons. As of July 2006, tips from viewers had resulted in the capture of 897 criminals and the live recovery of 50 missing persons. Felons caught as a result of Walsh's show include several fugitives from the FBI's Top Ten program (Chapter 7) and Robert List, a mass-murderer who remained at large for 18 years after killing five members of his family. List's arrest, 11 days after his case was featured on TV, demonstrates the media's power to reach every part of the world.

Fox executives canceled *America's Most Wanted* for six weeks in autumn 1996, replacing it with comedies, but protests from the public, law enforcement agencies, and government officials brought it back to life. Since October 2001, the show has also featured episodes profiling the world's most-wanted terrorists.

Success inspires imitators, including such local programs as *Capital Region's Most Wanted* (from Albany, New York), *Massachusetts Most Wanted* (Boston), *Metro's Most Wanted* (Des Moines, Iowa), *Michigan's Most Wanted* (Detroit), and *New York's Most Wanted* (New York City), all aired on local Fox affiliates.

some bandits responded violently to that interruption, new silent alarms were invented, linked to the nearest police station, FBI office, or private security company.

Today, most bank vaults include a variety of noise and motion sensors that sound alarms if burglars try to penetrate the door or walls. Similar systems are commonly used in museums and art galleries to protect precious artwork. The speed of official response to an alarm depends on the bank's location, time of day, and various other factors.

Gold bars in a safe deposit box. Safe deposit boxes provide added security inside vaults for customers that want to store items they feel are not safe elsewhere. *Matthias Kulka/zefa/Corbis*

Security guards, once common in banks nationwide, have vanished from most small branch banks with the advent of high-tech surveillance devices, but they are still found in some larger American banks and in many overseas banks. Modern bank guards are usually provided by private security firms and are not police officers. They may be trained with various weapons, but generally do not participate in bank robbery investigations. Each state has its own rules for training private security guards and the weapons (if any) they are allowed to carry.

During the 1920s and 1930s, bank guards were often heavily armed and equipped with quirky devices including bullet-proof cages and tear-gas grenades. They were seldom well trained, and often posed more danger to fellow employees and customers than any bandit gang. Some towns went further still, creating alert systems that rallied armed citizens to defend their banks against robbers. The results were often bloody, as at Northfield, Minnesota, in 1876, and at Coffeyville, Kansas, in 1892 (see Chapters 1 and 2).

Most bank guards today have been replaced by closed-circuit television (CCTV) and other surveillance devices that photograph bandits during a robbery. CCTV was first developed as a form of bank security, and then expanded into other realms of public and private security. Many homes today have their own CCTV, including "nanny cams" to watch babysitters.

Using computers, some modern bank robberies are accomplished from hundreds or thousands of miles away. That threat, in turn, has produced a whole new security industry dedicated to frustrating hackers or crackers who penetrate bank computer systems and illegally transfer funds from one account to another. Cases include

- Vladimir Levin, a Russian mathmetician who used the Internet to access the accounts of several Citibank corporate customers in 1994 and transfer $10.7 million to bank accounts established by accomplices in Finland, Germany, Holland, Israel, and the United States. British police arrested Levin at a London airport in March 1995 and delivered him to U.S. authorities for trial in September 1997. Levin bargained with prosecutors in February 1998, pleading guilty on one count of conspiracy to steal $3.7 million. He received a three-year prison term and was ordered to pay $240,015 in restitution. Citibank spokesmen say that all but $400,000 of the stolen $10.7 million was recovered.
- In August 2000 British police arrested three men for attempting to rob a London-based online bank, Egg PLC. Bank security officers traced the would-be robbers using special software and identified them to authorities. In accordance with British law, the three suspects were not identified in media reports.
- In March 2005 security technicians at SophosLabs announced that British police had foiled a plot to steal £220 million from the London office of a Japanese bank using "Trojan horse" software

to penetrate the bank's computers. Once again, no suspects were publicly identified.

- On December 14, 2007, police in Karnataka, India, arrested six persons on charges of stealing Internet banking identities from 115 persons in cyber cafes around Bangalore. Press reports identified the six as "Joseph," "Akbar," "Hamid," "Chandru," "Siddique," and "Y.K. Mani." Authorities claimed the defendants had stolen money amounting to 1.2 million rupees ($30,635) from 28 bank accounts in Bangalore, Delhi, and Mumbai since 2005.

Computer security systems operate on two basic levels. One protects against external threats, while the other monitors internal activity to prevent embezzlement (theft) by bank employees. A classic case involves the Bank of China's Kaiping sub-branch in Guangdong Province, which lost $500 million to dishonest employees in October 2001. The thieves fled to North America, where Yu Zhen Dong was captured in 2002. The others, Xu Chao Fan and Xu Guo Jun, have not been found.

ON THE ROAD AGAIN

Money is most at risk while in transit to and from banks. Since the Wild West days of stagecoaches and gold strikes, bandits have raided cash shipments regardless of risk. Modern outlaws, like those described in Chapters 8 and 9, continue that tradition.

Early transport security came in the form of strongboxes protected by armed guards. Wells Fargo (see Chapter 2) pioneered that system with its stages and foiled many holdups spanning seven decades. Careless bandits often died while trying to steal Wells Fargo shipments.

In the twentieth century, banks and transport companies introduced armored trucks to improve security. These vehicles include layers of armor resistant to bullets and some explosives, plus bulletproof glass and tires that do not burst when punctured. Inside, drivers and guards are well armed and linked to their base by cell phones and two-way radios.

As with any other security system, however, armored trucks are vulnerable to certain high-powered weapons. Modern bandits often strike during cash deliveries or pick-ups, when truck doors are open and members of the crew can be reached without penetrating the vehicle's armor.

IF IT HAPPENS....

Robberies happen, despite the best, most expensive security systems. In those cases, bank employees and police still have a few surprises in store for the bandits.

Dye packs are explosive devices filled with colored ink, inserted in bundles of money, called "bait money," surrendered to bandits during a holdup. Prior to robberies, the packs are stored next to magnetic plates that keep their triggers dormant. When removed from the magnetic field, the trigger is armed. A small radio receiver inside the dye pack then gets a signal from a transmitter near the bank's door, activating a timer. When the timer runs down, the pack explodes, permanently staining the cash—and sometimes the robber. Many dye packs also release a cloud of colored smoke.

Today, an estimated 75 percent of all American banks use dye packs, disguised inside bundles of real $10 or $20 bills. At press time for this book, dye packs were credited with helping to capture 2,500 American bank robbers, while recovering nearly $20 million. Today, global positioning system devices are becoming a new tool in the fight against bank robbery.

Police SWAT teams are trained to deal with hostage situations such as take-overs by armed bank robbers. As indicated by their name, they use equipment and methods beyond the normal capabilities of most patrol officers, including sniper rifles, high-tech surveillance equipment, and techniques for penetrating buildings under siege. The SWAT team's mission is rescue of hostages, but members are prepared to use deadly force if necessary.

STILL AT LARGE

On those occasions when bandits escape, investigation proceeds along parallel lines. Bank robbery is both a state offense and a federal crime (if the target bank insures its deposits with the U.S. government). Thus, local police and FBI agents may investigate unsolved cases. Since the terrorist attacks of September 11, 2001, the FBI investigates fewer bank robberies than in previous years, generally limiting activity to cases where thieves steal $100,000 or more.

According to the FBI's Web site (http://www.fbi.gov), bank robberies are the least common type of armed robbery in America, but bank bandits steal more than other thieves. In 2004, for example, police reported 401,326 robberies across the United States, only 9,632 of them involving banks. Those bandits stole an average of $4,221 each, with some taking much more (for a total of $70 million).

The good news is that bank robbery has a higher clearance (solution) rate than any other kind of robbery in the United States. Police catch 58 percent of all American bank robbers, versus the 25 percent catch rate of thieves overall. Only murder has a higher clearance rate among violent crimes, at 62 percent.

The media is a powerful tool for catching bank robbers. Surveillance photographs of unknown bandits frequently appear on TV news programs and are broadcast by Crime Stoppers units across the country. Crime Stoppers is an international organization that seeks to fight crime by enlisting the aid of the community in connection with law enforcement. Serial bandits who commit multiple robberies are more likely to be identified. Once names are matched to faces, the most notorious cases are sometimes featured on national programs such as *America's Most Wanted*, which has a long record of capturing felons at large through citizens' tips.

Chronology

1798 *August 31 Philadelphia:* Thomas Cunningham and Isaac Davis steal $162,821 from the Bank of Pennsylvania in America's first bank robbery.

1831 *March 19 New York City:* Edward Smith steals $245,000 from the Bank of Wall Street.

1852 *July San Francisco:* Wells Fargo's first office opens.

1866 *February 14 Liberty, Mo.:* The James-Younger gang stages America's first daylight bank robbery.

1876 *September 7 Northfield, Minn.:* Armed towns-people ambush the James-Younger gang.

1882 *April 3 St. Joseph, Mo.:* Bob Ford kills Jesse James.

1892 *October 5 Coffeyville, Kan.:* Townspeople wipe out the Dalton gang.

1922 *December 18 Denver:* Bandits steal $200,000 from an armored car outside the U.S. Mint, killing one guard.

1930 *December 16 Sidell, Ill.:* "Baron" Lamm and two accomplices die in a shootout with police after robbing an Indiana bank.

1933 *June 9 Indianapolis:* John Dillinger robs his first bank.

June 17 Kansas City: Five lawmen and prisoner Frank Nash die in the Union Station massacre.

1934 *April 22 Rhinelander, Wis.:* Two persons die in a bungled raid on the Dillinger gang at Little Bohemia Lodge.

May 18 Washington, D.C.: Congress makes bank robbery a federal crime.

May 23 Arcadia, La.: Police kill outlaws Clyde Barrow and Bonnie Parker.

July 22 Chicago: G-men kill John Dillinger.

1934 *October 22 East Liverpool, Oh.:* Police and FBI agents kill "Pretty Boy" Floyd.

November 17 Barrington, Ill.: "Baby Face" Nelson battles FBI agents, killing two and later dying from his wounds.

1935 *January 16 Lake Weir, Fla.:* "Ma" Barker and son Fred die in a shootout with FBI agents.

1936 *May 31 New Orleans:* FBI agents arrest Alvin Karpis.

1937 *October 12 Bangor, Me.:* G-men kill two members of the Brady gang, wounding and capturing a third.

1950 *January 17 Boston:* Thieves steal cash and securities valued at $2.8 million from a Brinks vault.

1952 *February 18 New York City:* Police capture Willie "The Actor" Sutton.

1965 *June 4 Big Springs, Neb.:* Duane Pope steals $1,598 from a local bank, shooting four employees.

1974 *April 5 San Francisco:* Heiress Patty Hearst joins the Symbionese Liberation Army in a $10,960 bank robbery.

September 27 Reno, Nev.: Thieves steal $1,044,000 from a local bank.

1977 *September 5 Chicago:* Unknown bandits loot the First National Bank of $1 million.

1978 *October 25 Los Angeles:* An illegal wire transfer lifts $10.5 million from the Security Pacific Bank.

1979 *March 25 New York City:* A wire-transfer theft removes $1.1 million from City National Bank.

August 21 New York City: Bandits steal $2 million from an armored truck outside Chase Manhattan Bank.

1981 *October 20 Nyack, N.Y.:* The May 19th Communist Organization takes $1.6 million from an armored car, killing a guard and two state patrolmen.

1983 *November 26 London:* Six robbers steal 10 tons of gold bullion, worth $45.5 million, from the Brinks Mat warehouse at Heathrow Airport.

1984 *July 16 Ukiah, Calif.:* Members of The Order steal $3.6 million from a Brinks armored truck.

1986 *April 11 Miami:* Bandits William Matix and Michael Platt battle FBI agents, leaving four dead and five wounded.

1997 *United States:* Bandits stage 8,372 bank holdups, killing 40 persons.

February 28 Los Angeles: Bandits Emil Matsareanu and Larry Phillips Jr. die in a televised police shootout.

March 29 Jacksonville, Fla.: Thieves steal $18.8 million from a Loomis-Fargo vault.

September 13 Los Angeles: Six bandits steal $18.9 million from the Dunbar Armored Company, the largest bank heist in U.S. history to date.

2000 *United States:* 7,546 bank robberies reported.

Italy: 2,464 bank holdups investigated.

2001 *United States:* 8,259 bank robberies reported.

2003 *New York City:* 408 bank holdups reported.

March 18 Baghdad: Hours after U.S. forces begin bombing Iraq, unknown thieves steal $1 billion from the Central Bank of Iraq, the largest bank robbery in history.

2004 *Los Angeles:* 537 bank holdups reported citywide.

2005 *August 6–7 Fortaleza, Brazil:* Burglars tunnel into the Banco Central, stealing currency equivalent to $69.8 million.

Endnotes

Chapter 2

1. Michael Newton, *The Encyclopedia of Robberies, Heists, and Capers* (New York: Facts on File, 2002), 261.

Chapter 3

1. Willis Newton and Joe Newton, et.al., *The Newton Boys* (Austin, Tex.: State House Press, 1944), xiii.

Chapter 4

1. Bryan Burrough, *Public Enemies: America's Greatest Crime Wave and the Birth of the FBI, 1933–34* (New York: Penguin, 2005), 32.

2. Michael Newton, 168

Chapter 6

1. Michael Newton, 281.

Chapter 7

1. Michael Newton, 247–248.

Chapter 9

1. Bradley Hope, *New York Daily Sun,* Dec. 29, 2006.

Bibliography

Beebe, Lucius, and Charles Clegg. *U.S. West: The Saga of Wells Fargo.* New York: E.P. Dutton, 1948.

Bruns, Roger. *The Bandit Kings: From Jesse James to Pretty Boy Floyd.* New York: Crown, 1995.

Burrough, Bryan. *Public Enemies.* New York: Penguin, 2004.

Edge, L.L. *Run the Cat Roads: A True Story of Bank Robbers in the '30s.* New York: Dembner Books, 1981.

Gibson, Walter, ed. *The Fine Art of Robbery.* New York: Grosset & Dunlap, 1966.

Helmer, William, and Rick Mattix. *Public Enemies: America's Criminal Past, 1919–1940.* New York: Checkmark Books, 1998.

Newton, Michael. *The FBI Encyclopedia.* Jefferson, N.C.: McFarland, 2004.

Newton, Willis, and Joe Newton. *The Newton Boys.* Austin, Tex.: State House Press, 1994.

Schultz, Duane. *Quantrill's War: The Life and Times of William Clarke Quantrill, 1837–1865.* New York: St. Martin's, 1996.

Sutton, Willie, and Edward Linn. *Where the Money Was.* New York: Viking, 1976.

Unger, Robert. *The Union Station Massacre: The Original Sin of J. Edgar Hoover's FBI.* Kansas City: Andrews, McNeel, 1997.

Wellman, Paul. *A Dynasty of Western Outlaws.* Garden City, N.Y.: Doubleday, 1961.

Wilson, Colin, Damon Wilson, and Rowan Wilson. *World Famous Robberies.* Bristol, England: Paragon, 1994.

Further Resources

Books

Kirchner, L.R., *Robbing Banks: An American History 1831–1999*. Cambridge, Mass.: Da Capo Press, 2003.

Newton, Michael. *The Encyclopedia of Robberies, Heists and Capers*. New York: Facts on File, 2002.

Swierczynski, Duane. *This Here's a Stick-Up*. Royersford, Pa.: Alpha Publishing, 2002.

Web Sites

Crime Library
http://www.crimelibrary.com

FBI History, Famous Cases
http://www.fbi.gov/libref/historic/famcases/famcases.htm

The FBI's Top Ten Most Wanted Fugitives
http://www.fbi.gov/wanted/topten/fugitives/fugitives.htm

Wanted by the FBI: Unknown Bank Robbers
http://www.fbi.gov/wanted/unkn/unkn.htm

Index

About the Author

A former public school teacher (grades 6–8, 1979–1986), Michael Newton has published 202 books since 1977, with 12 more scheduled for release from various houses through 2010. His first nonfiction book—*Monsters, Mysteries and Man* (Addison-Wesley, 1979)—was a volume for young readers on cryptozoology and UFOs. His recent reference works include *The Encyclopedia of Serial Killers* (2d edition, 2006) and seven other books from Facts on File (2000–2007), plus the *FBI Encyclopedia* and an *Encyclopedia of Cryptozoology* (McFarland, 2004 and 2005). His history of the Florida Ku Klux Klan, *The Invisible Empire* (University Press of Florida, 2001), won the Florida Historical Society's 2002 Rembert Patrick Award for Best Book on Florida History. A full list of Newton's published and forthcoming titles may be found on his Web site at http://www.michaelnewton.homestead.com.

About the Consulting Editor

John L. French is a 31-year veteran of the Baltimore City Police Crime Laboratory. He is currently a crime laboratory supervisor. His responsibilities include responding to crime scenes, overseeing the preservation and collection of evidence, and training crime scene technicians. He has been actively involved in writing the operating procedures and technical manual for his unit and has conducted training in numerous areas of crime scene investigation. In addition to his crime scene work, Mr. French is also a published author, specializing in crime fiction. His short stories have appeared in *Alfred Hitchcock's Mystery Magazine* and numerous anthologies.